MEMOS

FROM THE

HEAD
OFFICE

MEMOS
FROM THE
HEAD
OFFICE

CHANNELING THE MUSE IN

BUSINESS AND IN LIFE

PERRY MARSHALL

JOHN FANCHER

PLANET PERRY

Oak Park, Illinois

Perry S. Marshall & Associates
805 Lake Street
Oak Park, IL 60402 USA
www.perrymarshall.com

Although the author and publisher have made every effort to ensure that the information in this book was correct at press time, the author and publisher do not assume and hereby disclaim any liability to any party for any loss, damage, or disruption caused by errors or omissions, whether such errors or omissions result from negligence, accident, or any other cause.

Project Management by Marla Markman, MarlaMarkman.com
Book Design by Glen Edelstein, HudsonValleyBookDesign.com

Front cover photo: The window at Gallarus Oratory, Smerwick Harbor, County Kerry, Ireland ©2021 Perry Marshall
Back cover photo: Clogher Head, Ballyferriter, County Kerry, Ireland ©2021 Perry Marshall

Ordering Information:
Quantity sales. Special discounts are available on quantity purchases by corporations, associations, and others. For details, contact the publisher at the address above.

Publisher's Cataloging-in-Publication data

Names: Marshall, Perry, author. | Fancher, John, author.
Title: Memos from the head office : channeling the muse in business and in life / Perry Marshall; John Fancher.
Description: Includes bibliographical references and index. | Oak Park, IL: Planet Perry, 2021.
Identifiers: ISBN: 978-1-7354211-1-7 (paperback) | 978-1-7354211-2-4 (ebook) | 978-1-7354211-3-1 (audio)
Subjects: LCSH Business--Religious aspects. | Creativity in business. | Spiritual life. | Business leadership. | Executives--Conduct of life. | Businesspeople--Conduct of life. | BISAC BUSINESS & ECONOMICS / Decision-Making & Problem Solving | BUSINESS & ECONOMICS / Motivational | BUSINESS & ECONOMICS / Skills | BUSINESS & ECONOMICS / Small Business | SELF-HELP / Spiritual
Classification: LCC BF637.S8 .M37 2021 | DDC 650.1--dc23

978-1-7354211-1-7 (Softcover)
978-1-7354211-2-4 (eReaders)
978-1-7354211-3-1 (Audiobook)

Printed in the United States of America

For all those who endured the deafening silence
until wisdom broke through

CONTENTS

DOWNLOADS THAT CHANGE THE WORLD

J. K. ROWLING DIDN'T AGONIZE FOR years over the plot line for *Harry Potter*, as most authors do when they begin writing. She received the story as a mental download while on a stalled train in London. Over two to three hours, Rowling wrote furiously in her notebook as the information flowed. She then spent years editing and reworking those ideas into multiple books and movies, but the origin of one of the most popular fiction series in history came not from within Rowling but from the outside. From the Muse. From the Head Office.

Perry Marshall's reinvention of the 80/20 principle arrived in a 10-second flash of insight. A month later, after he had been searching unsuccessfully for the precise formula, a woman Perry had never seen in his life marched up to him and said, "You're working on a math problem. You need to keep working at it, because you're going to figure it out." He had been working on that very problem all day, yet had not mentioned it to anyone. This "memo from the Head Office" led Perry to write the world's bestselling book about online advertising,

Ultimate Guide to Google Ads. And his "fractal 80/20" formula took the entrepreneurial world by storm and was published in *Harvard Business Review* 12 years later.

"Can you get business advice from God?"

Or the Head Office or the Muse, or whatever words you assign to it?

The answer is an emphatic *yes*. And it's not just business advice. As you turn the pages of this book, you will meet many entrepreneurs and business owners who have real-world experiences of this and are already doing it. *Memos from the Head Office* chronicles the epiphanies, inventions, and course corrections of authors, innovators and entrepreneurs from all over the world. These men and women discovered that, on the journey to success, a listening ear can be even more valuable than a sharp mind or brilliant strategy.

HAVE YOU EVER IGNORED THE INNER VOICE?

WHEN I WAS A YOUNG SALES guy scrapping for every last purchase order, I had a side hustle in the evenings and weekends. One winter afternoon, I was planning a drive from Chicago to Indianapolis for an 8 p.m. business meeting with a promising individual.

A couple of times that day, a thought was nudging me, "You ought to call him to confirm before you head down." In hindsight, that thought seemed more from the outside than from the inside. Twice I dismissed it.

I drove three hours to Indianapolis. As I drove, snow flurries started to pick up.

The guy wasn't at the restaurant. I called him. "Oh, I am sooo sorry, sir, I totally forgot. This sounded really interesting, too. Look, it's already 8 p.m., I've got an early morning flight, and I'm really beat. Can we please reschedule? I'm really sorry, I hate standing people up."

I returned to my car and began the three-hour drive back to Chicago. But on my way through a parking lot, I hit a steep curb and blew out my rear tire.

I found the spare tire. Snow was falling steadily now. The spare was flat, too. When I tried to fill it, I heard the *psssssssst* of a puncture. I did not have money for a motel or tow truck.

I called every listing in town. Only one place was open at 8:45 p.m.—a truck stop on the south side of Indy. I managed to find a can of tire repair foam at a 7-Eleven and inflate my spare to the point where I could at least limp to the tire shop. Driving back to Chicago on a dinky little spare tire in snow was unthinkable.

I drove to the truck stop and purchased a brand-new tire on what room was left on my credit card. Then began the drive back. Snow was falling heavily now. Interstate 65 was layered with ice. If I drove any faster than about 35 mph, the ice would begin accumulating so thickly on my windshield that I couldn't see anything. I passed 50 cars that had spun into the ditch or median. I didn't get home until 3 a.m.

I had now expended 10 hours, a tank of gas and a new tire. I had risked life and limb, spent an evening away from my wife and baby girl and gone right back to work the next day on three hours of sleep. All because I didn't *listen*.

Ever ignored a memo?

This book is about not missing memos anymore—and getting more when you need them.

Untangling the Knots between the Spiritual and the Commercial

IF YOU ARE A PERSON OF conviction who runs a business, you may sometimes harbor complex thoughts, doubts and hesitations about fully throwing yourself into the demands of entrepreneurship. Some days you're not sure if it's OK to make a lot of money. You may be leery of the level of imbalance and eccentricity that startup businesses often demand. You might wonder whether your business completely aligns with your spiritual purpose.

This book aims to help you resolve some of the tension you feel between the spiritual and the commercial. The stories and examples in these pages demonstrate how you can tap into the extraordinary power available from the Head Office—the Muse—the Unseen Hand—God—the Divine—or whatever name you choose. (See Chapter 1 for more about the source and identity of this power.)

You will meet real businesspeople—many of whom run sizable companies or are captains of industry, shouldering tremendous responsibilities—who rely on the Head Office for guidance. In their stories, you will glean actionable advice about how you, too, can access that guidance.

Because if you believe that your plans are guided by a trustworthy unseen hand, you will be far more confident in the projects you undertake. If you expect to hear a gentle but unambiguous "no" when you're about to make a bad move, you will attempt fewer dead-end projects and eliminate some blind alleys. If you pay attention to the Head Office "memos," you'll have more wisdom in maneuvering the complexities of the real human beings you meet along the way.

If you're in business, cultivating your ability to listen is the ultimate "$10,000-per-hour skill." The storytellers in this book, who range from part-time "kitchen table" entrepreneurs and freelancers to executives in charge of billions of dollars of assets, have honed their listening ear. Enjoy their personal accounts and learn from them.

Full disclosure: I have been an online business consultant since 2001. Over that time, I have come to know thousands of entrepreneurs. Most of the storytellers in this book are from my "tribe." Some are only acquaintences but I've known some for a decade or more.

Also, as part of my monthly membership, I offer "Memos from the Head Office" sessions. Members can tune in to the call, state their first name, and receive a "memo" from one of my memos staff. Many of the people who tell their story in this book have participated in those calls. Gary Wilson and Julie Richards, as well as several other hand-picked people, have been delivering those memos to my business community for several years now. Several of the stories you will read in the book mention Gary and Julie, who have cultivated their listening and receiving skills diligently and humbly for a long time. I trust them to listen well for my members.

You will find lots of information about how to cultivate your listening skills in this book, but it is not a textbook. Although it offers tips, how-tos and some extensive commentary along the way, we primarily want the stories and storytellers to speak for themselves.

Stories communicate truth far better than lectures or sermons or textbooks.

Rather than approach this book as an instruction manual, we invite you to "go deep" with the stories that speak to your heart and mind. Read those stories more than once. Take notes. Ask "Is this something that I could do in my own life?"

The way you receive and perceive Head Office memos will be different from the way they are received by Perry and John or any of the storytellers in this book. So, this book can't give you a universal, step-by-step method to unlocking this form of communication. You need to make this process your own. Discover your own memo personality and open yourself to Head Office direction. We hope these stories will help you discover your unique path.

Chapter 1

MIRACLE ALGORITHM
DOWNLOAD

GARY KLOPFENSTEIN, CHAIRMAN of GK Investment Management, lives in Chicago's Gold Coast neighborhood. An extraordinarily successful business executive in asset management, strategic consulting and leadership development, he is former U.S. CEO of Berenberg, the world's second oldest bank. Before that, Gary grew assets under management for Mesirow Financial from $1 billion to $60 billion in less than 10 years.

Memos from the Head Office Resources

Detailed, up-to-date information about Gary and all contributors to this book is provided in Appendix 4, which is posted online.

A free online resource has numerous additional tools and information, including access to memo calls on a donation basis; a quiz called the Spiritual Perception Profile that helps you identify how you hear the Head Office; and additional stories and videos better delivered online than in book format. All of these are available for no additional charge at www.perrymarshall.com/morememos.

You probably would not expect a guy like Gary to be very "childlike." Yet I—Perry—can't think of many guys I know who exhibit more childlike principles related to Head Office memos. (Just a note here: Throughout the book, "I" and "me" refer to Perry, unless you are reading one of the book's first-person stories.) First, I'll let Gary tell you one of his most memorable experiences. And then I'll let him tell you what he does to hear more.

The Head Office Sent Me a Trading Algorithm While I Was Having Coffee with a Friend

From Gary Klopfenstein

I'm a professional currency trader. A few years ago, I tried writing an algorithm, a mathematical model to define currency risk.

The nuances in emerging market currencies make risk management tricky. I was hoping my algorithm would provide a more elegant means of controlling that risk at a lower cost than anything else available at the time.

I knew I was getting close to nailing it, but there was still one crucial piece missing. Anyone who does intense analytical work often hits that point. You work for hours, days or weeks, and you reach a point where you're just *stuck*.

The gears of your brain run out of grease. The whirring grinds to a halt, and you just know you're not going to get the answer by thinking harder. Forcing your brain to work just leads to stress, fatigue and depression.

I've learned to recognize that feeling. And that's when I know that the final pieces of the puzzle are going to come from *elsewhere*.

So, I had a feeling the Head Office was going to supply the missing piece. It wasn't going to be me. I just didn't know when or how Heaven was going to provide it.

While trying to hammer this out, I caught up with a friend for coffee. We talked about a lot of things. Algorithms and currencies never came up!

But right in the middle of our conversation, I saw something. I can't say it was a hallucination. I don't know if I actually *saw* it with my eyes, or it was just so vivid in my mind that it *seemed* like I was seeing it with my eyes.

But I saw a formula. A bunch of Greek letters and numbers.

I must have looked pretty strange when it happened, because my friend cocked his head to the side and said, "Gary? What's going on?"

I said, "Hey, I just got a download! I saw a formula in my mind. I think it's the missing piece to something I've been working on. It's the piece I've been waiting for!"

He said, "Do you need to write it down?"

I said, "Nope. I got it all in front of me in my mind."

When I got home, I did write it down. It was a formula used in other areas of math but had never been applied to the area I was working on.

I popped it into my formula, and everything worked perfectly. My completed algorithm defined risk in emerging market currencies. It was a breakthrough in our industry.

I now license this algorithm to companies outside the U.S. to help them manage currency risk. It's helped several companies make a great deal of money, likely tens of millions of dollars, as well as protected them from *losing* a great deal of money. So, it was a very practical memo from the Head Office.

And it came while I was having coffee with a friend. Wasn't thinking about formulas at all.

True Breakthroughs Often Come from Outside

Gary's experience is similar to a great many "breakthrough" ideas. Peter Ilyich Tchaikovsky said:

> The germ of a future composition comes suddenly and unexpectedly. If the soil is ready ... it takes root with extraordinary force and rapidity, puts forth branches, leaves, and, finally blossoms ... the main ideas and general outline of the work come without any racking of the brains, as a result of that supernatural inexplicable force we call inspiration.[1]

The American playwright Neil Simon once said, "I don't write consciously—it is as if the muse sits on my shoulder" and "I slip into a state that is apart from reality."[2]

The one thing I hope you get from this book is that receiving memos from the Head Office is not difficult. Yes, there are certainly things you can do to improve your listening ear, and we'll dive into those things headfirst throughout this book.

But if I could boil down this book to one sentence it would be: "Become like a child."

Childlikeness doesn't come easy for many entrepreneurs and professionals. Most of us approach our businesses and our lives with great seriousness. We study. We analyze. We create systems. We calculate. We draw detailed plans. There's nothing wrong with that.

But when it comes to hearing, analysis clogs the pipe. You will never capture the Muse with gritted teeth and furrowed brow. Gary has every excuse in the world to be a man of gritted teeth and furrowed brow! In fact for a long time he was that guy—until he tapped into his childish wonder and started honing his listening ear.

In the story above, the answer to Gary's problem—an old formula

---

1 *The Life and Letters of Peter Ilyich Tchaikovsky*, University Press of the Pacific, 2004.
2 Nancy C. Andreasen, "Secrets of the Creative Brain," *The Atlantic*, July/August 2014.

used in a new way—came from outside. That happens frequently. The answer, the missing puzzle piece, the revolutionary idea, comes from outside.

I've experienced this many times. When I'm trying to solve a business problem, for example, the "answer" will often come from outside of business channels—especially while I'm doing something that has nothing to do with business.

In 2018, I was prepping to speak at a seminar. People were traveling from across the world to hear me present for three days. Five weeks before the event, I was playing with my 7-year-old daughter when it suddenly occurred to me that a concept I typically explain by drawing a triangle would be much richer if I made the triangle 3D—a tetra-hedron. I scribbled the idea down on a piece of paper in my wallet and kept playing with my daughter.

The next day I began working on producing my idea. I found a company to manufacture and print these 3D objects for me. When I passed them out at the seminar, those little triangles were the hit of the entire event. Yes, it was geeky (no less geeky than currency trading algorithms!) but it literally added a brand-new dimension to an already powerful concept.

I've discovered the more you listen to the Muse, the more "symbiotic" breakthroughs you get. I think it's because the more atten-tively you listen, the more readily you receive all manner of connections. If you're open to such connections, they make themselves known to your subconscious mind—then they become conscious.

For Gary, being open to connections starts with having fun. Let him explain.

"Can You Give Me a Picture?"

From Gary Klopfenstein

Receiving memos is easier than you think. People try to make it difficult and mystical and magical. It's not. At least, it shouldn't be. It's supposed to be fun!

I ask people to just picture something that's easy for them to see, like your refrigerator or your favorite chair. Bring it up in your mind so you can see it clearly. Now just ask Heaven to give you a picture. Ask: "Can you give me a picture of something?"

Then, *do not* filter or judge or edit what you see. Just notice the first image that comes to your mind. Something will pop up. Just accept that the picture is from the Head Office.

Go with it. Then ask: "What does that mean?"

Then just listen. Again, don't filter, edit or judge. Then, pass on the information to the person you're with, saying, "I don't know if this makes sense but—"

It will almost always be something positive and loving. Sometimes prescient.

Many times I get so worked up and entangled in my problems and stresses that my "memos channel" gets blocked off. Usually it's because I'm looking for some *big* revelation. I'm waiting for some booming voice or looking for a crystal-clear vision.

And then I'll realize that a quiet voice has been whispering to me all along. In a still, small, simple voice. If I calm down for a bit and stop stressing out about the *big, important problems*, I'll hear answers to those problems.

DON'T MAKE IT SO HARD

Perry here. We humans are so bent on complicating things. Some of us believe memos need to be received in a mystical, mysterious process reserved for a select, holy, monastic elite. Some of us believe only people like Albert Einstein or J. K. Rowling can experience a thrilling epiphany.

That has not been Gary's experience. Nor mine. Nor that of any of the storytellers who appear in this book, as far as I'm aware. I am a thinker and my biggest obstacle is getting my brain out of the way. I'm also a writer and a strong editor. It took a long time for me to switch my editor off and just let words flow.

When you are listening to the Head Office, it is imperative that you do *not* edit, judge or evaluate what you are hearing in that moment. Also, do *not* wonder or worry about whether you're hearing yourself or listening to the Muse. This is critical because you can discern the source of the memo later. You will have the rest of your life to figure that out.

In a sense, it doesn't matter whether you are listening to yourself or to the Head Office. Because if you can't learn to listen to yourself, your channels will never get clear enough to listen to the Muse!

So there you are, writing in your notebook. Or maybe you're walking your dog or driving your car. You ask a question of the Head Office and you think you heard an answer—unless it was just a bad burrito?

You don't know! And you don't have to know! Not today anyway.

Just record the answer as accurately as you can and circle back later to consider its value and its origin. Remember, you might have the rest of your life to decipher it. You don't need to decide right now. Wisdom and insight come over time.

Register for a memos session and pick up your bonus
material and all appendices free at
www.perrymarshall.com/morememos.

Perry Learns to Switch Off His Inner Editor

From Perry Marshall

Just when I was beginning to explore the concept of Head Office memos, I went to a conference where I saw a long line of people waiting to talk to a couple named Ivan and Isabel

Allum, who were delivering memos to each one, rapid-fire, as fast as they could talk. You could almost say they were downloading each person's *Harry Potter* story and relaying it in real time, one after another.

There were at least 50 people in that line, and the Allums would give three to five minutes to each person. I knew some people in the room, but Ivan and Isabel didn't know any of us. But when I heard them talk to my friends and acquaintances, I could tell that Ivan and Isabel were hitting all kinds of things right on the money. Nailing stuff right and left. It was unreal.

The spiritual atmosphere in the room was thick with intensity. As long as I live, I will never forget the numinous presence, the palpable sensation of love I experienced in that room that evening. I suddenly burned with curiosity. I had to understand how they did that. So, a year later, I drove to a four-day training taught by the Allums in Stratford, Ontario.

During the very first hour of Isabel's workshop, she instructed everyone to write down their own name on a piece of paper, fold it up so their name was not visible, and pass it to the front. Then, the slips of paper were redistributed to the 60-plus people in the room who had come to this training from all over North America. Now we each had somebody else's piece of paper.

Isabel instructed, "Ask God to give you a message for this person. Whatever comes into your mind, *write it down* on your piece of paper."

This *shoved* me out of my comfort zone! I couldn't imagine anything more unnatural.

Man, this is so weird. This feels like jumping off a cliff with no net. What if I'm wrong? What if I'm just making stuff up?

It was utterly foreign to me to simply listen to my

intuition, completely *blind* like that. I didn't even know quite what I was supposed to listen to. I was terrified of sticking my foot in my mouth.

Plus, years of sales training were screaming at me: "You always *ask questions* and *listen* before you start telling people anything about themselves, Perry."

Don't forget: The general idea here was that whatever I wrote down on that piece of paper might be divinely inspired *and* if the other person has that kind of expectation, you don't wanna get it wrong! Yet I sensed Isabel wasn't putting that sort of pressure on us. We were just practicing. Memos kindergarten. OK, I'll follow Isabel's instructions: "Write down the first thing that comes to your mind."

I asked for wisdom. I began to notice my mind wandering, and it began to form a picture. I was going into a building and walking up a stairway immediately past the front door. At the top of the stairs, there was a table with windows around the top of the room. A blond woman was sitting at a table near a window. Sunlight was streaming through the window.

At this point, my mind picture seemed little different from what happened every day when my mind wanders. But I recalled what Isabel said: "Just run with the first thing that comes and write it down." I began describing the scene on the paper.

As I wrote, I realized that the woman sitting at the table at the top of the stairs was sad, very sad. She was writing in a notebook. There was a powerful sensation of sorrow coming from this picture.

I began to write down my impression of the woman. As I wrote, the impression became clearer. Finally, I reached an understanding: "God knows her sadness and he wants her to know that he knows. That he is there to comfort her."

That last insight was like the knowledge you have in dreams, where you just "know" something, even though you didn't see it and nobody has explicitly explained it.

That was all. I wrote the message, signed my name at the bottom of the paper, folded it up and turned it in. Isabel distributed the pieces of paper back to their original owners.

I hoped that my memo would make some sense to the recipient.

Five minutes later, a blond woman whom I knew only slightly approached me with tears rolling down her cheeks.

"Perry, did you write this?"

"Yes."

"You described every single morning for the last five years, in my morning meditation time, ever since I moved to the U.S. from the U.K. You described the nook where I sit, including the window and sunlight and the sadness and my notebook.

"Perry, I miss home so bad. I miss my dad desperately. You nailed it. There is *no way* you could have known this, but it is 100% on target."

Wow!

Isabel was right—this insight was available to everyone. Because if I can get a memo, anybody can.

And this was just my very first crayon drawing in Head Office kindergarten. The experience made me wonder what could happen if a person spent five or 10 or 20 years honing their listening ear. Then I realized that I already knew! I'd seen this skill in action when I watched the Allums delivering memos at the previous conference.

What an incredibly powerful way to edify and encourage my fellow travelers—simply hearing Heaven's words for another person and relaying the message.

An experience like this is unmistakable and life-changing. It was nothing like the performances I had seen on TV where some perceptive person or "psychic" read body language and groped around as they tried to guess what color dress your mother liked to wear. Seasoned veterans like Isabel and Ivan never groped around. They spoke without hesitation. Forceful and direct. Sometimes the words would stream faster than they could relay them.

My experience demonstrated to me that the lines of communication are open. The Power at the other end of the line wants to send you more memos. You don't need to work harder, think harder or retreat to a monastery for 10 years to get them. There is no special passcode to open the line. The line is open. The memos are on their way.

Who Should Be Reading This Book?

Dear reader, I don't know you. You might be Buddhist or Hindu or Muslim or Protestant or Catholic or a lapsed Catholic. You might be a New Age spiritualist. Maybe you're agnostic (which means "I don't know"). You could be Mormon or Jewish.

Maybe you've Lego'd together some hodgepodge of spiritual perspectives and experiences. Maybe your God is the "Higher Power" of Alcoholics Anonymous. (When my friend Paul Wendell Obis decided to stop drinking, he appointed Bigfoot as his higher power. Bigfoot reportedly sufficed for the first few weeks.)

Have you had horrific experiences with religious people and organizations? Join our club! (John Fancher and I detail some of our most sordid religious encounters in Appendix 1 at the end of the book.) Or perhaps you describe yourself as "spiritual but not religious."

This book welcomes readers from all the above categories and from any other spiritual designation you might choose.

I will be honest, however, and say this book is probably not for you if you're a devout atheist—if you're absolutely certain all supernatural notions are silly delusions. Similarly, if the story of my friend Paul and his Bigfoot-Higher-Power strikes you as highly heretical and causes your inner theologian to burn with rage, you also may want to take a pass on this book.

On the other hand, if you're the sort of atheist or person of faith who is alert to the possibility that you might be missing out on something, you may enjoy this book quite a bit. If you read with care, the detailed stories and verifiable details in these pages could vigorously shake your views.

These stories are documented. John Fancher and I personally know everyone you're about to encounter in this book. You can Google them and verify they exist. Appendix 4 (which is posted online at www.perrymarshall.com/morememos) gives you names, businesses and current websites. Quite a few of them, including Gary Klopfenstein, have enviable credentials and reputations to maintain. Their stories are true, and all the storytellers in the book are fully identified. There are almost no anonymous stories in this book. All we are asking is that you set aside your apprehensions and skepticisms and open your mind to the possibilities.

"OK, PERRY, BUT WHO ARE WE LISTENING TO, ANYWAY?"

In any case, you may be a little apprehensive about these discussions involving spiritual matters. And you may be wondering exactly who or what we're talking about or who or what inhabits this Head Office.

Perhaps most of us can agree that this incredibly beautiful world and exquisitely tuned universe surely came from something or someone very great. Most of us embrace the possibility that this being, this entity, is also the source of love and purpose in the world.

And human beings everywhere and in all cultures pray. Why? Because humans instinctively suspect that whoever or whatever created us can hear us—and maybe even reads our very thoughts. That transcendent being is what I refer to when I say "God."

You might be saying, "But I don't want my idea of God. I want the actual Head Office. Whoever and wherever that is. I admit that my idea of the transcendent, however lofty, can at best barely approach the real thing."

Regardless of religion or creed, can all of us at least agree on that? And if so, then we can also agree that our words are inadequate and that labels like Head Office, Muse, Divine, God (or, um, Bigfoot) will have to suffice, even though we know they are not perfect? In the same way, our discussion in this book about getting "memos" serves as shorthand for all the unexplained ways we can receive unusual communications or insights.

It's often not easy to talk about these kinds of topics. But if you're ever with people who feel truly safe sharing unusual spiritual experiences, you are likely to find that many individuals will relate truly mind-bending events and coincidences.

I think it's irresponsible (and, in fact, anti-science) to shrug off an experience as chance or accident. You don't get to ignore data just because it doesn't fit your pet theory about the world.

But in our age, sharing such experiences is often frowned upon. Stories like this are whispered to friends over morning coffee, not shouted from the rooftops. The "official" version of the world, according to "educated people," is that such things are impossible or sheer coincidence. So, people don't talk about them much.

But funny thing, not talking about these kinds of events doesn't prevent them from happening. I know numerous people who, even as small children, have always seemed to "know" things that they couldn't possibly know. (In Chapter 5, I review a range of scientific experiments that have studied premonitions and other such phenomena.) Most of these people were told they were crazy, so they stopped sharing their premonitions with others. But that doesn't mean they stopped having those experiences.

As with all forms of power there can be a dark side to these experiences, and the power can be abused. (See Appendices 1 and 2 for more information and cautionary tales.) But this book is not meant to explore every facet of every spiritual dimension. My purpose is to simply help you switch on your own channel to the Head Office.

Everybody who knows me or does business with me knows I'm a Christian. (See Appendices 1 and 2 for more information about my spiritual beliefs.) My customers and clients also know I'm at ease with people of many spiritual perspectives and paths. And I have personally witnessed people of every creed and religious belief get genuine, life-changing memos.

Access to a memos session and a "how do you
hear memos" conversation with Perry are online at
www.perrymarshall.com/morememos.

I am not writing this book as a way to convert you to my Christian creeds. But if you're not sure what to connect to, I'm offering to let you borrow my connection. "Whoever Perry is tapping into—can I get that?"

That's a good start. That will work.

So, your job, then, is to simply fatten the pipe and separate the signal from the noise. The first step is to become like a child, to expect magic, to delight in the expectation of hearing memos, to make it fun and to be playful and creative.

Other steps? We will dive into those in the next chapters.

But before we go there, let's hear one more cool story from Gary Klopfenstein.

I Pulled the Perfect Number Out of the Ether While the CEO Waited

From Gary Klopfenstein

I run a family office. That's financial speak for private investment fund that serves a defined set of clients. My business is investing in various other businesses. Most of them are private companies. I often take on an advisory role, such as a seat on their board of directors.

One day, I scheduled a conference call for the directors of one of these companies. For some reason, the CEO and I were the only two people who could make the call that day.

One of the questions we were trying to answer at that time was "What should the size of our next round of capital be? Or should we not raise any at all at this time?"

The CEO asked, "Gary, what do you think?"

In my mind, I asked the Head Office, "What's the right number?"

I received a very specific number. I repeated the number to the CEO.

He said, "Hmmm, that's about 50% more than I thought. But, OK, why do you think that's the right number?"

Again, I checked in with the Head Office in my mind. And immediately I got three reasons.

I can't reveal those reasons here because of confidentiality concerns. But the first two were perfectly normal strategic things that any board member might say to a CEO.

But the third reason was quite a stretch. It was just a number. $22.3 million. Providence told me this number would work if we plugged it into the formulas we were using to solve this business problem.

These formulas are long and complex. There's no way I could have figured out what number would "fit" on my own. Not without a computer. But I said, "I really think this number will work."

He said, "OK, well, I'll go back and run the models and see if it comes out. I'll let you know."

The next day he called. "Gary, that number you gave me fits exactly right. What you heard makes sense. So, we're going to take this valuation and go out to our investors."

The next week he elevated the capital raised to that number.

The Head Office gave me that number—along with three reasons that number would work.

There was no way I could have known that number would work. I had never seen their models. Yes, I would have known the numbers were wrong if they had been off by a factor of 10. But there's no way I could have come up with a number, that exact, off the top of my head.

Chapter 2

MY FIRST MEMO

From Perry Marshall

March 21, 2003, is burned into my memory. Richard Koch's book *The 80/20 Principle* had set my mind on fire just a few weeks earlier, as I had been struck with an insight: "80/20 isn't just a theory about 'Group A' and 'Group B'; it's a calculus formula. It's a ramp-like curve. It's infinite, and it's fractal."

I had been obsessing about the formula ever since. What's this formula? How would you set it up? How would you solve it? I was rolling it around in my mind, trying to figure it out when something else remarkable happened: I hosted a single teleseminar on March 19 that generated over $11,000 of sales in one hour, which, at the time, was an almost miraculous amount of money.

It got me wondering how I could use my business to help support a relative who was building a school in

Mozambique. At the time, Mozambique was the 18th poorest country in the world. Most people there existed on a dollar a day, and those kids where Alan was working had nothing.

So, I spent March 21, 2003, thinking about two things: 80/20 math and Mozambique.

That night my wife encouraged me to go listen to a musical performance at our church. I went, and I knew music was playing, but I was a million miles away—in la-la land, dreaming of 80/20 formulas and thinking about Mozambique.

Suddenly, out of the corner of my eye, I saw a woman making a beeline for me. I had never seen this woman before, but she marched right up to me, stuck out her hand, and said, "Hi, my name is Vivian, and the Lord gave me a word for you."

Huh?? I had heard of stuff like this but never experienced it.

She said, "The Lord told me that you are very, very good at math, and you are working on some kind of formula, some kind of equation. Some kind of —" she struggled to find the right word. "Invention." I looked around. How many people in this room were trying to solve a math problem—right that minute?

She continued, "And you're going to figure it out. You just keep working at it and keep working at it, cuz you're gonna figure it out!" She turned to walk away but wheeled back around suddenly. "Oh, and he told me something else. You want to support missions. God is going to bless your business so you can support missions."

OK. She got the math part right. Invention was even the right word for it. Not too many people listening to this hippie music gig could have possibly been inventing math formulas at that moment. But how did she know I had a business? And about the missions part?

I stared at her, overcome with emotion. I said, "If you only knew."

She flashed me the brightest smile, pointed up in the air and said, "He knows!"

Then she turned and walked away. Just like that.

I had heard rumors of such things, but this had happened to me. No honest statistician could chalk up to coincidence how perfectly this stranger's message aligned to my current life. It had to be a memo from the Head Office.

It was unmistakable. I had been entertaining doubts about God, but I was not so deep into abject denial that I could shrug this off as happenstance.

I continued to chip away at the calculation but kept coming up empty, over and over. I searched the web but couldn't find anything quite like what I was envisioning. I rolled it around in my mind. I'd work at it for a while, put it on the shelf, come back every once in a while and try again. Time passed.

Three years later, I was sitting in a Roundtable meeting, refereeing a dozen wooly entrepreneurs, who acted as an informal board of directors for each other. I was doodling on a scratch pad when—epiphany! Suddenly I saw how to set up the equations. The 80/20 Power Curve was born.

The formula went through several iterations. For years, I used it for myself and with clients to make predictions and solve problems. Eventually, it evolved into the 8020curve. com tool I unveiled in my book *80/20 Sales and Marketing*.

HITCHING A RIDE ON A SUPERNOVA

Figuring out the formula was only part of the memo Vivian passed on to me that day in March 2003. She had also told me that God was going to bless my business so I could support missions. A few months after that memorable evening, my business hit the proverbial "hockey stick." I experienced 500 percent growth in two years, a magic carpet ride with books selling like crazy and speaking invitations rolling in.

Much later, I remembered what Vivian had said that night and wondered "Did anything interesting happen that week?" I combed through some old emails and found one from the previous Tuesday from Ken McCarthy: "Perry, I need someone to speak at my seminar on Google AdWords. I think that person should be you."

At the time, Ken's System Seminar was action central of the online marketing space, a magnet for the best and brightest. The conference accurately forecast every major trend in internet marketing from email marketing to video to mobile.

I had never seriously considered writing about or teaching AdWords until Ken's invitation came. AdWords was new, and few people understood it. I wrote the very first version of the information that eventually evolved into the *Ultimate Guide to Google AdWords* and offered it at Ken's seminar.

Nobody at the time had any idea that this eccentric, idealistic company from Mountain View, California, was about to become the 800-pound gorilla of the internet. But shortly after that seminar, Google went supernova, and my career lurched forward. I never imagined that my new book would eventually become the world's best-selling book on internet advertising.

That one speaking invitation, which came three days before I met Vivian, put me on the map. I was prepared, I had honed my marketing chops, and my business exploded—just like she had predicted.

From that point forward, I understood two things:

1. You take care of the poorest of the poor and He's gonna take care of you.
2. When you need wisdom, *ask*.

At the beginning of my 80/20 book, there is a dedication: "To the Master Mathematician, and to Vivian." I'm thankful to Vivian for boldly stepping out and talking to a guy who thought she might be crazy. As for the Master Mathematician, he knows how to solve everything. He's also a Master Entrepreneur and CEO.

Do you need help growing your business? Just ask.

FAST FORWARD 15 YEARS

Harvard Business Review Italia published the math for the 80/20 Curve in June 2018. It was the first publication for my idea, and there's a surprising story behind this too.

Every morning, I spend the first hour of my day ("Renaissance time") free writing, using my journal as a place to ask questions, pray, and get myself sorted out before the day begins. Below is a photo of a page from my journal from August 30, 2013.

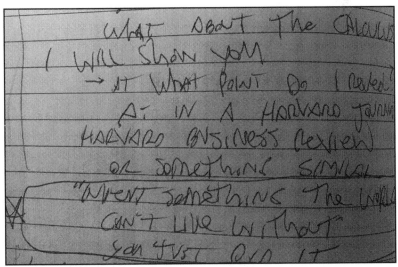

An entry from my journal on August 30, 2013.

In case you can't read my writing, here's a translation.

Q: "What about the calculus?"
A: "I will show you."
Q: "At what point do I reveal?"
A: "In a Harvard journal. *Harvard Business Review* or
  something similar. 'Invent something the world can't live
  without' [which is a goal that was written down on my
  bucket list]. You just did."

I had forgotten about this written exchange until I found it in late 2018 as I was looking through some old stuff. However, I had remembered the idea of waiting to publish it in Harvard's journal.

In 2017, Performance Strategies in Italy asked me to speak at its 2018 conference in Milan. I agreed. A few months later, they sent me an email: "We're featuring all of our speakers in *Harvard Business Review Italia*. Would you like to write an article for *HBR*?"

Yes, of course I would. I included the 80/20 Curve math formula in the sidebar. Around the same time, I got an email from an engineer at NASA's Jet Propulsion Labs at CalTech in Pasadena. He said he was teaching the 80/20 Curve in a productivity course and was asking for permission to use graphics from the book, which I was happy to provide.

Both of these completely dropped in my lap. Just to be clear, prior to this invitation, I had zero connections to *Harvard Business Review*. The HBR world pays no attention to mine and vice versa. My publication was certainly one of the most serendipitous things that have ever happened to me.

So now that I have described some of my most startling messages, let's explore how you can start receiving your own memos from the Head Office.

Participate in a live memo session and access supplemental
videos at www.perrymarshall.com/morememos.

Chapter 3

How to Get More Memos

THE STORIES YOU'VE READ SO FAR in this book have been included to help convince you that real, rational people get memos from the Head Office. And that those memos can help you solve difficult problems or provide you with unusual insight or encourage you during a difficult period. Now we want to help you cultivate the ability to hear the Head Office. It is the most valuable sensitivity you can cultivate in your life.

First, you must cultivate the ability to hear yourself. Let me tell you another story. Be patient, cuz this is a bit of a stir fry, but I promise it's all going to come together in the end.

A Singing Problem

From Perry Marshall

A few years ago a lot of midlife stuff was coming up for me. It was a dreadful period in my life. I started to notice that every time I tried singing along with a group of people, I would feel sad. I could be at a baseball game singing the national anthem, and I would get a lump in my throat and a feeling of being held back, dragged down.

I realized that this feeling had been with me for a long time and that it was showing up more and more. Something was up. Finally, it occurred to me that I might want to find out what the feeling was about and whether I could get rid of it.

So, I decided to employ a special technique I had learned from Abby Rohrer, a specialist in obsessive-compulsive disorders. She had explained to me that a lot of the stuff rattling around in our heads (and our hearts) simply comes from not knowing how to listen to ourselves and showed me a method to combat this problem.

In this technique, sit down with a notebook and write down a question you want to ask yourself. Write the question with your dominant hand. In other words, if you're right-handed, write it with your right hand. But put the pen in your "wrong" hand before you record an answer to the question.

Abby explained that the mental effort required to write with the wrong hand ties up the logical part of your brain. That logical side has been overpowering and drowning out emotions, but when your logical brain gets distracted, those emotions can be released. Writing with the wrong hand literally gets you in touch with the weaker side of yourself. The one you've been ignoring.

This is important! "When you record your answers to yourself," Abby said, "you must write down whatever comes to mind, no matter how irrational or nonsensical it seems. Just follow it."

So, with my dominant hand, I wrote: "Perry, why do you feel that lump in your throat?"

Then I moved the pen to my other hand and began to scrawl out an answer, trying to let go of any preconceived notion of what it might be.

As I did this, I began to see a mental picture of an embankment next to a highway. I immediately thought, "This is stupid; what does this have to do with anything?" But I followed Abby's advice and kept going.

I started writing. In my mind's eye, I saw grass in a ditch, then pavement and a white line at the edge of a highway. Then I saw the highway, and then I saw it.

A dead cat. Smashed totally flat.

It was Mitsy, the cat we had when I was 6 years old. Shortly after Mitsy had a litter of kittens, she vanished. A few days later, we discovered her two blocks from our house, flattened on the highway. Bits of fur fluttered in the wind. I was heartbroken.

The instant I saw the dead cat in my imagination, I also felt that lump in my throat, that sickening feeling of sadness.

The same feeling I had been getting whenever I was singing. Identical. Apparently, I was still upset about my dead cat.

I asked Abby what to do with this information. She said, "It's real simple. You were sad about your cat, Mitsy, but you didn't let yourself grieve.

"So, Perry, the next thing for you to do is 'finish the feeling.' You just need to finish processing the feelings you had about your cat. Take yourself back into that emotional space of being 6. Go ahead and feel all the feelings you didn't let yourself feel back then. Feel them until they go away."

So one morning, before I climbed out of bed, I just lay there and traveled back in my mind to being 6 years old. I fully remembered once again what it was really like when we discovered Mitsy's body. I put myself right back into the middle of that sensation and experienced it very intensely for a while.

Then, after about 15 minutes, the feeling passed. It was as though the sadness just evaporated. I felt a sensation inside, like separate parts of my heart were melting back together. And then I was done.

I have never felt that sadness again. Now, singing the national anthem at a baseball game feels great.

ABANDONING THE MENTAL BAGGAGE

I had been carrying that sadness around for more than 30 years and never knew why. That memory and that unfinished emotion had been "burning CPU time" in my mind and body for decades.

My body was trying to tell me, but it took a long time before I finally listened to myself. The day I gave myself permission to grieve, I discovered unprocessed emotions can hang around and chew up resources for decades!

Never feeling sad while singing the national anthem was not the only benefit I gained from this experience. It wasn't even the most important one. Getting past the grief of this one particular experience also lightened the overall load on my mind and spirit. One less piece of mental luggage to drag around.

Think of how an Ironman competitor gains speed and efficiency by shaving ounces off of their racing bike, replacing lightweight parts with even lighter and more aerodynamic components. Think of how you gain internet speed when you delete programs running in the background on your computer. You thought you needed faster connection speed, but you really just needed less spyware.

That's what has happened to me as I've gotten rid of emotional junk. It has sharpened my sensitivity and intuition and improved my performance as a writer and business professional.

Nondominant Handwriting

The exercise I described is called nondominant-handwriting, and it is described in the book *The Power of Your Other Hand* by Lucia Capacchione. This could be a very useful exercise to help you open up your inner communication channels.

As I described above, you should use your dominant hand to write a question to yourself, such as "Why do you feel that lump in your throat?" or "Why are you having such a hard time making that phone call?" or "Why can't you get started on this project?"

Then switch the pen to your other hand to record your answers. Write whatever flows into your mind. Do not judge it, do not edit it, do not "think about it" and do not try to make sense of it. Just let it come.

Your rational mind will usually try to interrupt. You have to ignore that. Simply relax and write down whatever comes to you, as soon as it comes to you. Don't give a thought to what it means. It may not make sense at first. Half of it might be gibberish, but that's perfectly fine.

For me, words sort of dribble out like toothpaste coming out of a tube. It can be remarkably similar to that picture and message I got for the sad woman from the UK. You just have to write what comes. Many times it doesn't really make sense as it is coming, but just trust it.

It's a way of getting your inner control freak to step back and just "flow" with what is really going on inside of you and outside of you.

LEARNING TO HEAR YOURSELF

I shared my Mitsy story with you to help you understand one key point: You will never hear God if you're so emotionally puckered up that you can't even listen to yourself!

Nondominant-handwriting is just one of many techniques you can use to help open your emotional, intuitive and spiritual channels so you can hear everything that's being said. So your "sixth sense" has permission to speak up.

No doubt you're wondering "How on earth can I possibly know whether I'm listening to Heaven, when Perry just gave me advice on listening to myself?" Stick with me for a bit longer, and I think it will all become clear.

My mom suffered from bipolar disorder. I believe one of the reasons she struggled with mental illness for 30 years is that she always was an intuitive person, and potentially a prophetic person, a "seer." But her intuition was ignored, suppressed, belittled and abused her entire life.

Most people I grew up with were terrified of their intuitive side, which is why they were so uncomfortable with my mom. The folks at our church weren't going to approve of anything that didn't fit into their carefully manicured "systematic theology," which also managed to eliminate the voice of the Holy Spirit from the equation. How this made logical sense to them, I do not know. But I digress.

In other words, my mom never found her "tribe." Nobody really understood her. *Nobody* accepted this part of her until very late in her life. Only when she found some acceptance did she begin to improve.

Mom and Dad would be driving home from a party and she'd say, "That person doesn't like me." Dad would reply, "Oh, Betty! Your radar is always cranked up to 10. You are just imagining." I'm certain sometimes Dad was right. This is the downside of intuitive people. They are *too* intuitive sometimes. But not always.

Often, highly intuitive people think they're crazy, because they "know" things no one else seems to know. But by the time they're 4 or 5, they've learned it's better to shut up and keep that unknowable stuff to themselves.

I inherited some of my mom's intuition, but I too shoved it down. I did not begin to actively heed that inner voice until I was in my 30s.

For example, when my friend Bill tried to recruit me into Amway, I immediately sensed something was off. I clearly recall the uneasy feeling. I even remember thinking that the people who made the tape

Bill gave me were from a separate organization from the head company. A fact which proved to be very important later.

Nobody had even remotely told me any of this. I just intuited it. But I could not explain my reservations, and the "logic" of everyone's explanations made sense. So even though my gut regularly and repeatedly objected, I signed up. Then I wasted six years of my life trying to make it work. I never really got anywhere in that business.

This is surely one of the reasons why I was never successful recruiting people into the business. Although one side of my brain passionately believed in what I was doing, the other side harbored deep reservations. My inner editor managed to silence that side very effectively, but people sensed my ambivalence, no matter how much I tried to hide it.

Further along in my career, I learned to become aware of the signals in my body, literally paying attention to my "gut."

One day, I was on the phone with a guy who was pitching me a new idea. It made logical sense, but because my new awareness of my body, my intuition intervened. "Hey Perry, your stomach doesn't like this guy." That awareness helped my brain get into the conversation too. "Pay attention. Do you notice how this conversation is making you feel?"

I got off the phone as fast as possible. I needed no further explanation or inquiry. My body is almost always right in these situations, and I've paid a huge price for ignoring it. I've learned my lesson now, thank you very much.

All this goes in the stir fry.

A wonderful book, *The Artist's Way*, by Julia Cameron can serve as a field manual to teach you how to open your intuitive channels through daily journaling. To create great art, you have to be in touch with your intuitive side. The book is a manual for how to spend your Renaissance time, holding that open space in the morning before you engage with the world.

The method explored in *The Artist's Way* advocates free writing regularly (with your dominant hand unless you have a special reason to channel your weaker side). Let your thoughts flow freely. Don't edit. Don't try to compose perfect sentences. Don't judge what you're writing. Just let your thoughts flow effortlessly from brain to paper.

WHAT DOES GOD'S VOICE SOUND LIKE?

As you'll learn in the book you're holding now, if you want to pray—and hear back clearly—you should be relaxed, free of judgment and connected to your intuitive side.

Everybody prays. Even atheists pray every now and then, just in case. But notice that our book changes prayer from merely issuing requests to a conversation. Which is a pretty big deal.

Isabel Allum, whom you met in Chapter 1, taught me many things about opening up this conversation with God. One of the first things she taught me was that God's voice sounds almost like your own voice inside your own head. Very, very similar. But not exactly. Because God's voice says different things.

Another way to recognize God's voice is to determine whether the messages sound like something God would say. Saint Paul said, "But the fruit of the Spirit is love, joy, peace, patience, kindness, goodness, faithfulness, gentleness and self-control" (Galatians 5:22, World English Bible).

So, if the voice inside your head is resentful and not loving, dark and judgmental instead of joyful, angry instead of peaceful, temperamental instead of patient, mean-spirited and not kind, bitter instead of good, disloyal instead of faithful, harsh instead of gentle, erratic and impulsive instead of self-controlled, then you can know: It's not God who's talking to you.

Whenever someone says "God talks to me," many people get nervous. They associate such "messages from God" with terrorists and cult leaders. But that's like saying "Gasoline reminds me of arsonists and Molotov cocktails." Yes, gasoline can be put to really bad uses. But I still use gasoline as fuel for my car.

If you're ever confused, go back to the love, joy, peace, patience, kindness test. Memos from the Head Office are never used to control other people. They are given so we can work on ourselves.

As I surrounded myself with people who listened to God's voice, the most important thing I learned is that he's not judging us. He's not accusing us. He's not pissed off. He's not criticizing us. He's not glowering or looking down on us with anger and dissatisfaction. No! God's in a good mood.

I'm not saying God isn't upset about some things that go on in our world or that he approves of hurtful things we do. I am saying that the instant we're willing to surrender our egos and relax our clenched fists, he is utterly and fully willing to embrace us.

He's the best dad you've ever seen anywhere, always believing the best about His kids and doting on them. Always and without exception. He's the dad you always wanted. *Always* eager to help us pick ourselves up, go on and leave the past behind and renew and reinvent ourselves.

INTUITION AND GUT VERSUS HEAD OFFICE

Your stomach literally has hundreds of millions of neurons, and your gut really can "think." That's very useful information, but some of us ignore that knowledge, and we pay a price for it when we do. Intuition is similar. Our unconscious mind has tremendous ability to make connections that our conscious brain cannot make by itself.

Many of the smartest people I know deliberately harness these abilities. My business mentor Richard Koch, who's a billionaire, loads business questions into his subconscious and heads out on a three-hour bike ride every day. He relies not only on formulas and principles, but also on gut and intuition to make investment decisions. His net worth speaks to the power of his process.

Dan Kennedy, the legendary marketing genius, often talks about instructing his subconscious to solve problems while he sleeps. He wakes up with answers the next morning.

Those processes, the free writing practices described in this chapter and the numerous other exercises you can use to foster your inner voice are priceless. And you should, by all means, cultivate those skills.

But this is not a book about intuition and gut feelings. This book is about listening to the Muse, the Head Office, the Greater Power outside of yourself.

Cultivate the ability to distinguish your own intuition from the still small voice of the Head Office. Being able to make that distinction is one of the most valuable forms of discernment you can ever master. It takes focused effort, practice and guidance from others who have cultivated these gifts.

In other words, keep reading.

Join a live memos session and get resources for sharpening your intuition at www.perrymarshall.com/morememos.

Chapter 4

Dodging the COVID Market Crash

From Shanyn Stewart, a tax strategist who operates a tax planning and financial advisory firm called Advanced Accounting in Lambertville, Michigan. Over the next few pages, she describes some of her superrational encounters.

I'm an enrolled agent with a master's degree in forensic accounting. So there is a big part of me that is very rational. Logical. By the numbers. But there have been many moments in my life when I didn't know the answer. Times when my logical, rational mind reached the limit of its ability. Times where I have exhausted my brain trying to find the answer and found none.

I'm sure you've had many times like this in your life. Times when things don't make sense. Times when bad things happen to good people. Times when there does not seem to be any justice in the world. Times when the world seems random, chaotic, and not subject to rational laws.

During these times, I've learned to let go. To listen to the "irrational" voices of the universe. Sometimes a better word may be "superrational."

The following is a story about a few of those superrational encounters.

Sidestepping the 2008 Crash

I manage investment portfolios for some of my clients.

During the second week of August in 2008, I had strange dreams three nights in a row. Each night, I had dreams of markets crashing. I concluded that the Head Office was telling me to pull my clients out of the market.

So, on September 18, I advised my clients to pull out of the market and convert their assets to cash.

The stock market crashed 11 days later—on September 29, 2008.

Dodging the COVID-19 Market Crash

In January 2020, I had similar recurring dreams again, three nights in a row, and once again concluded that the market was about to crash. I spoke to my money manager on Tuesday, February 18, 2020, regarding potentially unstable market conditions.

And once again, I advised my clients to pull out of the market and convert to cash. A number of them followed my recommendations.

The first tremor in the markets occurred on February 20, when the coronavirus really hit Europe. The pandemic slammed the United States in mid-March, and then the markets went into in free fall for about two weeks.

Well, guess what? On March 5, 2020, the regulatory body that governs my industry notified me that I was being investigated. It said:

As of the time of this writing, June 2020, my clients are up appreciably.

NASDAQ OMX Group, NASDAQ Composite Index [NASDAQCOM], retrieved from FRED, Federal Reserve Bank of St. Louis; https://fred.stlouisfed.org/series/NASDAQCOM, January 6, 2021.

> [Our compliance department] has identified some of your advisory accounts in a quarterly review for cash held in advisory accounts. Over the last few years this has been an exam priority for both our internal supervision and the SEC.

What they were saying was they didn't like my accounts being converted to cash. A series of phone calls and meetings with the regulator ensued, beginning May 7, 2020. Those conversations went something like this:

> "Ms. Stewart, we have noted that in 2008, just before the Global Financial Crisis, you converted your clients to cash. We see that once again in 2020, just before coronavirus, you once again instructed your clients to exit the market. We are commencing an investigation to understand which information you obtained that led you to advise your clients in this way."
> "God told me to get my clients out of the market, so I did."
> "Ms. Stewart, you are not allowed to dispense financial advice based on that kind of information."

"Ma'am, when God tells me to do something, I do it."

"Ms. Stewart, this does not conform to legal standards or best practices of the financial industry."

"Well, I followed the instructions I got from the Head Office and my clients' portfolios are now up."

What's the Lesson from All This?

Every day, in some big or small way, you're going to be faced with a situation where your rational powers exceed their limit. I would never suggest that you should abandon your rational powers. That would be silly. Your life would be a mess.

But we all encounter problems that human wisdom cannot solve.

Maybe it's an argument with your spouse. Maybe it's a difficult teenage child. Maybe it's an unproductive employee. Maybe it's a thorny business problem. Maybe a terrifying health issue.

Whatever it is, in that moment, you have some choices.

One choice is to say "Well, I can't figure this out on my own, so I'm going to give up for now, come back and think about it more later."

That only kicks the can down the road. The same problem will be waiting for you when you return. And it will probably be bigger, thornier and more difficult.

Another choice is to reach out for help from the usual rational sources. And you should reach out to professionals for help. That's what they are there for. Got a legal problem? See an attorney. Got a financial problem? See an accountant. Got a health problem? See a doctor.

I'm a big believer in seeking rational, professional, expert help whenever possible, and I'm always the first to seek such help in any given situation. God wants us to be a body, a community. We are stronger together than alone.

So, reach out!

But sometimes you reach the limits of rational help.

At that point, you should choose the option most people ignore, the one many people don't believe even exists. Reach out for superrational help.

This choice is uncomfortable. Our Western minds chafe against it. We're afraid of looking foolish to our rational friends.

We're also afraid of reaching into the superrational and finding nothing. We're afraid of being disappointed. We're afraid God doesn't listen to us. We're afraid the universe is just a meaningless mass of swirling matter that doesn't care about our puny human problems.

Let me reassure you: He listens. The Divine does care a great deal. Fear not and reach into the superrational.

WILL THE HEAD OFFICE SOLVE ALL YOUR PROBLEMS?

Perry here again. Stories like Shanyn's are very puzzling to some people. After all, if the Head Office can tell you when to get out of the stock market, then why can't it solve all your problems?

Please notice a few things from Shanyn's story.

The Head Office did tell her to get herself and her clients out of the markets before they crashed—*twice*. The Head Office has warned her about innumerable other mistakes and pitfalls as well. These stories would easily fill a book or two, and maybe someday she'll write one.

But the Head Office did not stop some of her clients from ignoring her advice. Nor did the Head Office prevent Shanyn from getting hit by COVID-19 either! She was in pretty bad shape for a couple weeks during April 2020 and even made a couple of trips to the emergency room.

In the famous biblical story of Joseph (presented on Broadway as *Joseph and the Amazing Technicolor Dreamcoat*), God told Joseph exactly how to prepare for seven years of famine, but he did not prevent the famine. He also didn't intervene when Joseph's brothers sold him into slavery or step in when Joseph was sent to prison as the unfortunate victim of an overzealous Egyptian #metoo case.

But while Joseph was in prison, he cultivated his channel with the Head Office, as well as his skill in interpreting dreams. (People have been having prophetic dreams for a very, very long time.) And in the end, it all turned out all right.

BITTER DISAPPOINTMENT

Have you ever been sucked into the despair of utter exasperation when you felt like your prayers were bouncing off the ceiling?

You prayed for an uncle, an aunt, a grandpa or a child who was ill. Your prayer didn't get answered the way you wanted it to. The loved one died. You felt engulfed in a sea of hopelessness.

Maybe your prayers weren't about life and death. Maybe it was a "lesser thing," like getting a business off the ground. I tried to get a business project to work for years. I begged and pleaded for help from the Head Office, but it never went anywhere. A total bust.

But you only have to experience *one* undeniable miracle, and then you *know* the Head Office is in your corner. After that, there is no going back.

And it's imperative that you know this: Your channel to the Head Office is a *relationship*. It is not a series of transactions.

If your primary purpose in cultivating your listening ear is to get stock trading signals, you are trying to "game the system" of the Divine, and it is going to backfire sooner or later.

If, however, your primary purpose in cultivating your listening ear is to equip yourself for wise living and to love and serve other people, then, whether you hear the details exactly right or not, your life cannot help but flow in a positive direction.

Please also notice that I could just as easily say "If, however, your primary purpose in cultivating wealth is to equip yourself for wise living and to love and serve other people."

Can you see that wealth makes you powerful, and connecting with the Head Office gives you power? Can you see that power is good when used to serve other people and that power is bad when it's only used to serve yourself?

Can you also see that the Head Office gives us humility, because receiving memos makes it all the more obvious how much we don't know?

The Head Office does not exist to prevent you from having problems but rather to train you to solve bigger problems.

Also, I have never found the Head Office to be a substitute for:

- Discipline
- Research
- Finding and cultivating friendships
- Accurate numbers and figures
- Testing and experimentation
- Healthy habits and lifestyles
- Developing your talents and skills

Nothing of the sort! Memos are a catalyst for all of the above. To think otherwise is to abdicate your own responsibility for your life.

For a deeper dive into Memos and an interactive quiz that will

clarify how you best hear the Muse,

visit www.perrymarshall.com/morememos.

Chapter 5

IS THERE HARD SCIENTIFIC EVIDENCE FOR MEMOS?

HOW DID VIVIAN KNOW I WAS working on a math problem, even though she didn't know me from Adam? Has anyone formally investigated claims that you can actually know stuff you're "not supposed to know"?

How did Shanyn Stewart know the stock market was going to crash, days before it crashed, in 2008 *and* 2020? Is the world just physics and blind forces? Or is there evidence for another dimension?

I got in a smoking-hot argument with my brother Bryan about this very question around 2005. Once a missionary in China, Bryan had by then abandoned faith entirely. With that, he had also parted with the idea that prayers get answered or that any sort of "paranormal" activity occurs in the world.

His reasoning was persuasive. But I still wasn't completely convinced. My Vivian experience had taken place just a year earlier.

Yet, Vivian's predictions had not come to fruition at that point. I had not yet figured out the 80/20 formula. My business had grown but hadn't gone supernova. I was still intrigued by the extreme weirdness of meeting Vivian in the first place, but I knew that wasn't going to be persuasive to Bryan. And that was just about it for me, as far as personal experiences went. Any other encounters were from second-hand knowledge or things I had read about in books.

Bryan argued, "Perry, everything of that sort is all placebo effect, self-fulfilling prophecies, hoaxes or people manipulating the data. But when you chase it down, you'll always find a big puff of smoke."

Bryan's skepticism suddenly catapulted this issue lurking in the background, rarely getting my attention, to the forefront of my mind. My radar switched on, and I started hunting high and low for evidence either way.

PEAR Research Opens My Eyes

Not long after my discussion with Bryan, I got into a conversation with Howard Jacobson, a longtime colleague and author of the book *AdWords for Dummies* and numerous health-related books. Howie, who has a PhD in history from Princeton University, told me about unusual research at Princeton devoted to studying just this sort of thing.

For 28 years, the Princeton Engineering Anomalies Research (PEAR) program conducted research on questions like mine, and the book *Margins of Reality* by Robert Jahn and Brenda Dunne documents a wide range of those studies.

In one experiment, they dropped small balls through the air onto a pile, arranging for the balls to naturally form a symmetrical bell curve shape as they rolled down to the resting position. The purpose was to see whether a human observer, merely by concentrating, could deflect balls to the left or right. Moving objects through concentration is called "telekinesis." Repeated experiments across a long time verified that yes, some human observers can shift the trajectory of falling balls slightly to the left or right. They can measurably change the shape of the pile as the balls accumulate.

Another set of experiments tested perception from long distances. This is called "remote viewing." A pair of subjects would meet, then separate. The first would go somewhere and "send" pictures to the second person, who would then draw the picture on a piece of paper. The Princeton researchers devised clever criteria for objectively measuring how accurate the received picture was, compared to what was sent, and they demonstrated consistent ability to correctly transmit geographical information.

Similar research was done by Stanford Research Institute (SRI), which used remote viewers to report the location and configuration of Soviet military stations during the Cold War. The CIA released the following statement on June 6, 2003:

> These experiments were conducted under controlled laboratory conditions at SRI with several remote viewers whose perceptual abilities have been developed sufficiently to describe correctly and often in great detail geographical or technical material such as buildings, roads and laboratory apparatus. The phenomenon investigated was the ability of both experienced and inexperienced subjects to remote view geographical locations up to several thousand kilometers distant from his or her physical location.

> An increase in the distance from a few meters up to 4000 km separating the subject from the scene perceived does not in any apparent way degrade the quality or accuracy of the perception. The accumulated data concluded that the phenomenon is not a sensitive function of distance and that it is possible to obtain significant amounts of accurate descriptive information about remote locations.

> The experiments were conducted by the use of double-blind protocols which ensures that none of the persons in contact with

the subject can be aware of the target. The results of all sessions were recorded on a master log and all data associated with a given experiment remain unedited.

Some areas of physics are currently being explored as a possible explanation of the phenomenon itself.[3]

I interviewed Brenda Dunne, who ran the PEAR lab (you can listen in the online supplement at www.perrymarshall.com/morememos) and learned that she felt the veracity of their research was beyond question. But since these phenomena are without scientific explanation, most people preferred to ignore the evidence rather than acknowledge the existence of unanswered questions.

The Princeton studies found human subjects could nudge the outputs of random number generators up or down by small amounts by concentration, indicating mind/machine interactions. They also found that subjects could predict events before they happened. In other words, a recipient could receive an accurate picture before the sender transmitted it! This is called "precognition." They repeated these tests until the data indicated reliability with 99.999% statistical confidence.

When I first read *Margins of Reality*, I thought to myself "Most of this book is so boring, nobody could possibly have made it up." The majority of the book details the scrupulous design of experiments to isolate the specific variables in question. The procedures are painstakingly exact.

I found the last parts of the book, however, absolutely fascinating and insightful. They pointed out that rank-and-file scientists avoid asking such questions, but the very best and most forward-thinking scientists, such as Albert Einstein and Niels Bohr, were intensely interested in such mysteries. They imposed fewer boundaries on their thinking.

---

3 "Full text of "STANFORD RESEARCH INSTITUTE CONTRACT 8681 PARANORMAL PERCEPTION (AIRRS LIST SHOWS FOLDER IN BOX 1)." Internet Archive. Accessed Feb 5, 2021. https://archive.org/stream/CIA-RDP79-00999A000300100034-4/CIA-RDP79-00999A000300100034-4_djvu.txt.

Why Most Scientists Can't Buck the Status Quo

I encountered resistance similar to that reported in *Margins of Reality* in work related to my 2015 book, *Evolution 2.0: Breaking the Deadlock Between Darwin and Design*. The central theme in the book is that DNA is a code, and codes are designed. But rather than insisting that DNA must therefore be designed, as many religious people do, I decided to organize a multimillion-dollar technology prize and offer it to anyone who could get a code without "cheating."

I raised millions of dollars. Then I sought out professional scientists who could act as judges. Even though the prize requirements were crystal clear, and the principles uncontroversial, recruiting scientists was quite difficult. The subject of life's origin was simply too controversial for most scientists to risk being associated with the effort, so rank-and-file researchers declined.

The ones who did agree, interestingly, were 100% top leaders in their fields. Denis Noble is the guy who discovered the cardiac rhythm that made pacemakers possible. He has a Commander of the British Empire Medal from Queen Elizabeth and is an eminent physiologist. Denis was very enthusiastic about the project.

So was George Church of Harvard and MIT. George is the most influential genetic engineer of our age. *Time Magazine* voted him one of the top 100 people of 2017. George and his lab were featured on the TV program *60 Minutes* in 2019.

When I recruited George, I told him, "Do *not* do this if you don't like controversy." I couldn't help but smile when George replied, "Perry, I'm trying to build Jurassic Park and resurrect wooly mammoths at Harvard. Don't worry! Everything I do is controversial."

In 2019, we raised the prize amount to $10 million and announced it at the Royal Society in Great Britain. Once I had advocacy from the oldest scientific body in the world, it suddenly became much easier to get engagement from professional scientists.

Continued on next page.

An unfortunate discovery I made in the process of funding this prize is that science is extremely political. Most rank-and-file scientists literally risk their careers by challenging the status quo and espousing controversial views. The only people who enjoy the freedom to challenge the status quo are outsiders like Elon Musk, plus a very few science rock stars who have such enviable track records that no one can easily take them out. The rest are advised to keep their heads down and not rock the boat.

My experience is that average scientists tell you what they know. Extraordinary scientists tell you what they don't know.

Princeton University's PEAR lab, recognizing that we do not understand how these phenomena work, nevertheless endeavored to quantify their effects and correlate them with input conditions. Experiments were conducted with extreme care, and the bar for proof was high. But the odds that their results were "luck," and not a systematic process, are less than one in 100,000. There are currently no scientific models for how this works, so popular publications simply act as though such phenomena don't exist.

Paranormal research also attracts fierce opposition from skeptics. If you search online for the Stanford experiments, the PEAR lab or similar topics, you will quickly encounter tremendously vitriolic accusations that this is all "pseudoscience" and "woo-woo."

Some people are categorically opposed to entertaining dialogue about a whole constellation of subjects, including religion, life after death, prayer, healing, holistic medicine, homeopathy, Chinese medicine and chiropractic care. Many others are sufficiently intimidated to either believe the doubters by default or avoid the subjects entirely.

The media don't help either. It would be naive to say "If telekinesis actually works, how come it's not front-page news?" Controversies are rarely treated fairly. If it doesn't fit a prescribed narrative, you're not going to see it in the mainstream media. There are certainly facts established far beyond question (i.e., gravity or the periodic table), but a good deal of what most people think of as "science" is really just marketing.

It takes courage and resources to perform this kind of research. Please keep in mind that a scientist or technical specialist who risks career and reputation to advocate views that are out of the mainstream has far more skin in the game than the skeptic who tries to tear down the work.

DECIDE FOR YOURSELF!

Instead of simply believing me or the skeptics, I encourage you to do the research for yourself. Read books such as *The Conscious Universe* by Dean Radin and *The Field* by Lynne McTaggart. Follow the references they provide. Read the hundreds of scientific papers they cite. Read the reports of the thousands of experiments conducted over 100 years and check every reference to your heart's content.

In September 2010, *Southern Medical Journal* published the "Study of the Therapeutic Effects of Proximal Intercessory Prayer (STEPP) on Auditory and Visual Impairments in Rural Mozambique." Twenty-four people were tested, and the hearing of Deaf subjects improved by 10 to 60 decibels, while vision of some of the blind subjects also improved, ranging from zero improvement to significant improvement.

The book *The Miracles* by Dr. H. Richard Casdorph medically documents 10 miracles. Each chapter is a case study of one miracle, including doctors' reports, X-rays, etc. It reports ailments like huge tumors, multiple sclerosis and cancer vanishing completely, complete with medical documentation. If you're the least bit curious, go ahead and buy the book.

With my own two eyes, I've seen two Deaf people get their hearing back after 30-plus years without hearing. I report a half dozen miraculous experiences I've personally documented at www.coffeehousetheology.com/miracles.

The Miracle Detective by Randall Sullivan is a riveting account of a *Rolling Stone* reporter who decided to do an in-depth study of supernatural claims. *Testing Prayer* by Candy Gunther Brown, Ph.D., explores what is known scientifically about miracles and prayer. If you would like a solid academic and scientific exploration of this topic, Brown's book is a great place to start.

Lourdes, the Catholic pilgrimage site in southern France, has produced hundreds of documented medical healing reports. Dozens of books and medical studies have been produced, and you can find a generous sampling of them on Amazon and Google Scholar.

In *Medical Miracles* by Dr. Jacalyn Duffin, an atheist physician at Queen's University in Ontario, recounts her experience of studying bone marrow samples in her hematology lab when she was shocked to find that a patient had miraculously recovered from severe acute leukemia. This launched her on a journey of meticulously investigating 1,400 cases of documented miracles. Her book is published by Oxford University Press and outlines the stringent evidence required by the Catholic church before a miracle can be classified as "official."

Heaven is for Real, by Todd Burpo and Lynn Vincent, documents the story of 3-year-old Colton Burpo, who went to the emergency room with appendicitis requiring emergency surgery. Colton described leaving his body during the operation and going to heaven, specifying events and people that seemed impossible for him to have known about. Examples include knowledge of an unborn sister miscarried by his mother and identifying deceased relatives in family photographs, including his great-grandfather who had died 30 years before Colton was born.

The documentary film *Send Proof* by Elijah Stephens chronicles Stephens' personal search for definitive answers to these same questions, and he interviews several of the people I've mentioned here, along with famous skeptics like Michael Ruse, James Randi and Michael Shermer.

The books, articles and films I've mentioned here barely scratch the surface of a large body of literature. If you are tempted to categorically dismiss all forms of "the miraculous," first lay your hands on every one of these books and studies I've listed. Follow the footnotes to other literature. Do not stop until you have obtained an explanation that satisfactorily accounts for these events and phenomena.

Personally, I view both memos from the Head Office and miracles as an advanced technology that lends itself to experimentation—not some utterly separate "spiritual" phenomena that are somehow beyond investigation. And even though we do not understand why or how these things work, evidence is more than sufficient to establish beyond doubt that they occur.

Get a personal live memo session, additional memo
stories and a listening tip sheet at
www.perrymarshall.com/morememos.

Chapter 6

MIRACLE ON THE
FAX MACHINE

*From Susan Kruger Winter and her husband, Brian, who
live in Michigan. They are entrepreneurs who sell study skills
curricula to school districts and other educators.*

We were recovering from very damaging sabotage from a
once-loyal employee. (It appears her home environment
changed dramatically, and she took it out on us.) It was a
terrifying, messy, and incredibly expensive process to rebuild.
But we did it, thanks in large part to two beautiful souls we
hired during our recovery process.

But six months after we hired them, sales inexplicably
dropped. Our business is seasonal, and we were already "living
on a prayer" as we limped our way into the next season. But
two months into what should have been our most profitable
time of the year, sales were down by a terrifying 70%.

Once the inevitable was obvious, I went to the local
monastery—the tallest point in my county—and stood on top
of the hill overlooking all of Oakland County. I looked up at

the crucifix and screamed at God, "Why are you doing this? After all we've been through with our team, why are you taking these beautiful people away from me?"

I swear, I heard a voice say, "I wanted them to learn from you and take it to other places."

I totally thought I was hearing things, and that answer certainly did nothing to make me feel better. Was I just rationalizing my miserable situation?

I was sick to my stomach all night and into the next morning as I drove to work, knowing we'd have to let these two lovely people go.

We broke the news to them, and they took it so well. Said they knew it was coming as we had been fully transparent about everything. They knew we had done all we could do. Tears were shed and hugs exchanged. It went as beautifully as something that ugly could go.

By 9:30 a.m., it was over. The emotional toll of letting them go was so draining, all I could do was sleep. I told my husband, "I've got to take a nap. We can figure out how to redistribute work when I wake up. For now, I have to sleep."

Forty-five minutes later, while I was napping, a fax came in. It was a purchase order. A very large purchase order. Three times the largest P.O. we had ever received—enough to make up the 70% drop in sales.

A. Total. Game changer!

We thought about calling them back to work. But that memo from the day before held me back. Was it true? Is this really what Providence wanted? Ultimately, we chose not to call them back.

But two days later, I did tell them about the memo I received at the monastery. (We had always talked openly about such things, so I knew they would be receptive.) I sent them a text explaining my argument with God. I did not yet tell them about our "miracle purchase order," but I explained, "If what I heard was from him, then I encourage you to be on the lookout for leadership opportunities in your new job."

Meanwhile, back at our office, we almost immediately discovered something surprising: We had rebuilt our business with so much automation and efficiency that we didn't need the additional employees anymore!

Of course, we never would have let those two employees go if circumstances had not governed it; we always have projects waiting to be done. But our general operations were humming along so smoothly that we no longer needed the additional help.

Finally, six months later, I sent each of our former employees a letter, telling them about the "miracle purchase order." In the letter, I said, "I hope this means he was looking out for you, providing for you and guiding you to a better place. Well, I guess that's inherent in what we all believe. But my hope is that you *felt* his provision for you."

Both immediately responded, one with a three-paragraph text and one with a three-page letter. Both confirmed that they felt the layoff had been perfect timing.

The change had occurred at the top of the summer, and both had faced special circumstances with their children that required their full attention through the summer. Having that time (and the unemployment benefits) had turned out to be critical for their families.

And both confirmed they had landed happily in new jobs, with new leadership responsibilities. Each told us that they qualified for their new jobs only because of work experience they had gained with us.

Perry here again. I've known Susan and Brian since 2007 when they came to a small private workshop at my home office. That same week, Susan had quit her job as a schoolteacher to run their growing business. Brian was still teaching in the public schools.

I've watched them maneuver multiple personal and business reinventions. Like most small-business owners, they've often stared down some difficult choices. They've been angry at the Head Office more than a few times.

They are in the business of "study skills," but their true mission runs far deeper than that. They are really endeavoring to repair the torn fabric of a desperately broken and dysfunctional public education system. They are taking on the Big Monsters of the world.

I have learned that whenever people attempt to perform a job that theoretically should be easy (after all, many problems in these huge bureaucracies are plainly obvious), in reality, it can take 20 years to move the football five yards down the field.

It's like trying to change a deeply dysfunctional family situation, such as an alcoholic father and enabling mother, multiplied by 100,000. There is always a tremendous force of negative energy around these systems. Attempt to change such systems at your extreme peril.

Now, if you're truly assigned to carry out work of this kind in your life, even my above warning won't stop you. And it probably shouldn't.

But in my opinion, the only way you will succeed in performing work like this is if you have the Head Office behind you. And even then, the task is going to be more like Frodo carrying the ring to Mordor in *The Lord of the Rings* than a jaunt to the convenience store. Which is to say, this has been as much a spiritual journey for Susan and Brian as a game of business, marketing campaigns, curriculum development and sales chops.

Work like this attracts saboteurs. So, it's not surprising to me that one of their employees jacked up their customer relationship management system and it took a year and a half to discover the problem.

It's also not surprising that in the story above, things didn't move forward until Susan had reached a point of total surrender.

Read on for more such accounts because the next two chapters involve multiple stories of surrender.

Get my recommended reading list, access to live memos, tutorials and videos, and the story of Princeton's research into anomalous phenomena at www.perrymarshall.com/morememos.

Chapter 7

A Hard Rain's Gonna Fall

THE NEXT FEW CHAPTERS INCLUDE STORIES of multiple people who got memos from the Head Office in a variety of ways. They are presented without a lot of comment because I want the stories and the authors to speak for themselves.

From Chauncey Hutter Jr., who is is a tax marketing consultant in Charlottesville, Virginia.

I used to do seminars in cities across the country for accountants and tax professionals. My company offered coaching and advisory services. One particular weekend around 2010 was over-the-top successful. We did about a half million dollars in sales. Knocked it out of the park. It was the high point of my career at that moment.

We went out to dinner to celebrate. We were at the restaurant. Everybody was laughing, whooping it up and having a good time. I was sitting across from a buddy of mine, and, toward the end of the evening, he went white as plaster. He leaned over and said to me, "I gotta tell you something."

He said: "The Lord just told me that you're about to go through a very hard season. Your business is not just going to decline—you're going to be in real financial trouble. But Jesus is with you. It's gonna be hard, but he's got you."

I was floored. "What are you talking about? We're kicking butt. Look what just happened; everything's going great!"

But he just shook his head.

My messenger had been a very good friend for years. He was on staff at the International House of Prayer and was part of my prayer team for the "bonus sessions" at my events. He would pray for my clients. I trusted this guy. I knew 100% that he wanted only what was best for me.

I don't think I had ever received a "negative" memo from the Head Office before. I was used to messages being positive and encouraging. So, I didn't know how to receive this one.

Fast forward six months. My business was still doing great, and I was about to bring on a guy I believed would be really good for my clients. I invited him and his wife to have breakfast with me and my wife.

After the breakfast, my wife got in the car, looked me dead in the face, and said, "Don't do business with him. He's all talk, no action."

I hired him anyway.

You can probably guess what happened. He was all talk and no action, exactly as my wife had predicted. I gave him access to all of my top clients, but soon everything started to unravel. A few months later, I was sending massive refund checks to previously good clients.

Relationships in tatters.

Reputation tarnished.

I nearly became an industry pariah.

Over the next three to four years, my whole business nosedived. I had grown a multimillion-dollar business and made many of my clients millionaires. For years, I was Midas; everything I touched turned to gold.

But for the first time in my life, things weren't working. At all. And I didn't know what to do.

As money spiraled down the drain, I fired my staff. I gave up my office and worked from home. I cut expenses every way I could. But still the money ran away.

Spiraling Down—and Down Some More

For a while, we kept our million-dollar home, but eventually we couldn't even afford to have people over for dinner. We'd serve noodles, butter, and a can of beans. It was humiliating.

We couldn't go out with friends either because we didn't have the money. If we went to the local high school football game, we couldn't afford to buy our kids a hot dog.

We finally had to sell the house and move into a rental house. We shoved a ton of stuff into a storage facility. But then we had to move to a smaller place.

And then an even smaller place.

God just kept stripping us down, down, down.

And he kept stripping me down spiritually. This situation was getting me down to the basics, to what was truly important. Tearing away at my pride. Pulling me down off my pedestal.

I realized that I had been my own God. Fancied myself as the big dog, the guy that makes it all happen.

But all that eventually crumbled. It didn't happen in a weekend. It happened over many years.

The end came when I was standing in line to pay for groceries and the cashier said, "I'm sorry, sir, the card has been declined. Do you have another way to pay?"

I did not.

Everyone behind me was staring. I could feel their eyes on my shoulders. The cold sweat ran down the middle of my back.

It broke me. It brought me to the end of myself.

Finally, I said, "I can't do this. God help me."

And that's exactly where he wanted me—on my knees asking for help. And that's when the little miracles started.

People would show up on our doorstep with food. Money would show up out of nowhere precisely when we needed it. Barely saving us from missing rent. Barely saving us from getting our power shut off.

And, the humility, the brokenness I felt, led me to open up to my wife more, pray with her more. To have deeper, more meaningful talks with my kids: "God is good. He will provide."

This utter reliance on provision also gave me new empathy for people who were struggling. Anyone struggling. Even my clients. I had new eyes to recognize the look of anguish and shame when they were struggling financially because I had struggled that way too.

But God wasn't done with me yet. He wanted to make sure I got the message deep down in my heart, so he made sure I got it in my heart, literally.

Just as I was starting to "get it," my doctor said, "Chauncey, you're about one stroll to the mailbox away from a heart attack."

I went in for a stress test and completely failed. Two days later, a triple bypass. Followed by another heart procedure every year for the next three years. Ever try to run a business while getting your chest ripped open every year?

OK, I get it, God. You want my *whole heart*.

Eventually things started to turn around and then to move very fast. I started a new business that I tested with a part-time employee. We generated a quarter million dollars in sales in three months.

I've got plans to scale up another new business that could quickly be an eight-figure business enterprise, but I don't want to spout off about it. I just want to quietly get behind it and do it. My advisory business has been growing; I'm speaking at seminars again. Things are looking very strong. Big chunks of money.

God is good.

Another Memo from My Friend

I was talking with my old friend about 10 years after he gave me the "bad news," and he got an odd look on his face again. He leaned over to me and said, "Do you remember that word I gave you about how things were going to go bad in your business?"

I said, "Uh, yeah, I do."

He says, "I hear this now: It's over—the season is over."

It felt great to have him come back 10 years later, and tell me, "This is the season where you're going to expand, grow and have a significant, financial increase in your companies." He had just bookended my memos.

I think memos from the Head Office are not about someone "reading your diary." They're not about spiritual fireworks or bells and whistles.

They are about intimacy and immediacy. Memos prove that God knows you. And knows what's best for you.

He knew my business needed to go down for me to rise again even higher and better. I'm closer to him now. I'm closer to my wife now. I'm closer to my kids now. I'm closer to my clients now because of that memo.

I'm better for that "bad" memo. I'm better for going through that "hell." I have a whole different perspective on how I walk out my days now. I truly try to "abide" in his presence, as described in John 15.

I used to be the life of the party. I used to be Driven with a capital D. I used to be the guy with all the answers. Listen to me! Even my prayers back then were probably, "Listen to me, God, this is what I want you to do!"

But now I know prayer and relationships are way more about listening than talking. I'm paying attention more. I am opening my mouth far less.

Hey, if you're skeptical about this memo stuff, that's entirely OK. Just remember that you are your own best prophetic voice.

When you read Scripture or engage in any kind of spiritual practice, pay attention if something *zings* you. Start asking about it. Take out a notebook, write out your questions and wait. Listen! Then write what you "hear." Have that dialogue. Walk into the Head Office and have a meeting with the CEO. You can hear God for yourself without going to somebody else.

You will get an answer. You will get a memo. And you won't be able to deny it. You won't be skeptical anymore.

Chapter 8

STOLEN GEMS

From David Stanley Epstein who is a gem merchant in Brazil.

Thirty-eight years ago I moved to Brazil and became a gem merchant. When I moved to Brazil, I had no friends in the business. No relatives in the business. Not even enemies in the business!

I had to learn the hard way. All by myself. No outside help. I worked until my fingers were numb, trying to make a name for myself.

And I did.

Eventually I was giving lectures around the world. Then I wrote the only book on how to be a gem merchant.

I was, and still am, considered the best teacher of the gem trade in the world. I've lectured at the most prestigious institutes, including the Gemological Institute of America, the International Gemological School and the Beijing University Geology School.

In my little world, I was, and still am, well known. By 2007 I was riding high. That year I attended a large loose-gem show in Tucson, Arizona. The show was nothing special. Same as many others. But as I was packing up, I did something stupid.

Remember, I'm a gem buyer. Gem buyers pay very close attention to detail, especially when it comes to *security*. It's what we do. If you're not a detail-oriented person, you just cannot be a gem merchant! It's that simple.

And yet, as I was packing up, I went to the bathroom and left my gems unattended!

I *always* pack the gems first. *Always*.

I *never* leave gems unattended. *Never*.

Except that time. And I have no idea why. This was not just stupid. It was breathtakingly preposterous.

When I came back from the restroom, my gems were gone.

I've often thought back on that day and wondered, "Why did I do that? Why did someone as careful as me make such a stupid security blunder?" I essentially lost my life savings. I had gotten married about three months earlier, and now I had nothing!

My trade is capital intensive, which means you have to have money to make money. So, I was, at least for the foreseeable future, ruined.

All I had left were some loose stones that were not worth much.

And this was in 2007. If you recall what happened in '08, you know things did not get much better for me, money-wise. Like many others, my industry clenched its collective fist, and everything tightened and dried up.

What Are Your Options?

So, there I was, a renowned gem expert—busted. And nobody would help.

I was calling everyone I knew and offering any discount I could think of for counseling, teaching, anything to try to scrape together some money. Nothing worked. Every single response was *no. No. No. No.*

I reached a point where I had nobody left to call. No ideas left to pursue. No favors left to call in. I was out of options. I had never been more desperate or despairing in my life.

When I was at my lowest point, my wife, Julia, of less than a year came up to my office. She saw the agony on my face and said, "Well, why don't you ask God to help you?"

I was born into the Jewish religion. As I grew up, I started to ask questions and not just blindly accept my ancestors' faith. For most of my life, I had been an agnostic. I did not know if I believed in God or not.

I had too many questions, such as: "If there is a God, what is his nature? Did he create everything and then step back and watch, like someone peering through the glass at an ant colony? Or was he personal? Did he interact with us in some way?"

But if there were a God, how could I have the audacity to ask him for anything after he had given me everything I had? How could I be so selfish to ask for more?

That's what I told my wife. "How can I ask someone who's given me everything to give me more?"

She said, "Well, maybe he likes you to ask. Maybe he'd be perfectly happy to help. Like a father might for a son."

"Gee, I don't know if I can do that," I said.

She waited. She let the silence hang for a moment, then asked, "Well, what other options do you have?"

I don't know what my face looked like as I peered up in her eyes, but in my head, I heard this profound message: *Duhhhhhhhhhhhhhhhh!"*

Eventually, I nodded slowly. "I see your point."

And right then and there, we held hands and prayed. I think I probably started with something like, "Um, please excuse me for asking for anything else, God, after you've given everything in the universe, but I'm desperate."

We finished our prayer, and my wife went back down to her work. Twenty minutes later, the phone rang.

The caller on the other end said, "David, I need your help. Could you please help me fill this order?"

For a few seconds, I didn't say a word. I remember holding the phone away from my face and staring at it for a few seconds.

Then I said, "Sure. What do you want?"

The caller needed loose, crystallized, well-cut, Brazilian center stones. These stones have light coming out of them. They're not opaque. They are used in rings, pendants and earrings. And those stones were nearly the only thing I had left in my inventory.

I hung up the phone and looked around in a daze. I don't believe in coincidences, so this was a moment of revelation.

I looked up and said, "OK, I believe. I believe you're here. I believe you hear, you see, you feel. I believe you made everything in the universe. I believe nothing was before God. Everything was made from God. Everything is God."

Those words may sound a bit strange, but that was the conclusion I had reached. We are the essence of the mind of God.

I accepted God as personal at that moment. And the phone rang again.

This caller also wanted loose, crystallized, well-cut,

Brazilian center stones. Exactly what I had in my minimal inventory.

I said, "Thank you very much, God, but you didn't have to do that for me to believe you. I believed you. I will believe you the rest of my life. There's no stopping. I'm in. OK."

But he (by the way, I think God is neither masculine nor feminine; I just use "he" out of habit) wasn't satisfied. When I came to the office the next morning, I got yet another call for loose, crystallized, well-cut, Brazilian center stones.

Exactly what I had in my tiny remaining inventory.

Three times a coincidence?

Now, I know there are people who will say that it was a coincidence.

Maybe once. Mayyyyybe twice. But three times?

It's not a coincidence when it's *exactly* what I had in my minuscule inventory all three times. I've been doing this too long. That *does not happen.*

That was no coincidence.

It would not have been more convincing to me if the third caller had said, "Hello, my name is God. Can you fulfill this order?" God wants us to know that he is omnipresent, but beyond that he wants us to know he is personal.

He's right by your side, cheering you on, and willing to offer a helping hand if you need it.

When I go to sleep at night, I thank God for the day he gave me and ask him to protect me at night. When I wake up, I thank him for protecting me and renewing my energy.

I talk to God, and I ask him to direct me on the course he would like me to take in order to make him happy.

I don't know what reason you have for not asking him for help, but I know this: Your reason is not valid. Don't do it all yourself. He can't wait for you to ask for help.

Chapter 9

DON'T LET NOAH DIE

From Jackie Macedo, a cook, internet marketer and single mum who lives in Sydney, Australia.

I was a Christian from early childhood and a churchgoer at times in my life, although a cynical and cerebral one.

But the only "spiritual" experience I ever had was when I was in college in 1992. My sister was attending the University of New South Wales, and she invited me to a Christian conference being held there. It was vaguely charismatic, but, honestly, I don't remember much about it today except for the title: "God Is in Control."

I think the speakers were trying to dole out some peace of mind to college kids stressed out about what to study, who to marry, what career path to take. I wasn't too worried about any of that, but somehow those four words just got imprinted on my heart. I cannot explain it.

God is in control.

Anyway, other than that experience, my "faith journey" was pretty darn dull. I got married. And then divorced.

And that's when I lost the plot. Completely.

When my first marriage fell apart, my faith community really let me down. I expected support and comfort during my trials. I mean, isn't that what a faith community is for? Instead, I got abandonment, derision and scorn.

So, I was out. Check, please! Those hypocrites are the most judgmental people on earth.

I eventually got remarried. But he left me while I was pregnant with my second child!

I went alone to the "gender reveal" ultrasound appointment. But I got more than that. I got news that would change my life forever.

The doctor looked at me gravely and said: "Jackie, based on the ultrasound, it looks like your baby has a heart defect and bowel defect. Either of these alone would indicate Down syndrome. The fact that they are both present makes it a near certainty."

I was at the 20-week mark, which meant I had only four weeks left to legally terminate the pregnancy. The doctors pressured me to make a decision that day or to proceed with an amniocentesis to confirm the diagnosis.

I said, "No, that's all I need to know today. Thank you." I decided in my heart, "My baby has Down syndrome, and I'm going to prepare myself for that."

Still beating quietly in my heart were those four words: God is in control. It had been years since I had thought of those words, but now they flashed up bright and vivid.

Not My Choice

I decided, "Whatever happens with my son, whatever the outcome, I will accept it. I'm not going to play God and decide whether or not he lives or dies."

Over the next weeks, I got a lot of subtle (and not-so-subtle) pressure to terminate the pregnancy. Because I was going through the public hospital system in Australia, I would see a different doctor each time, and each new doctor would pressure me to go ahead with the tests. I kept refusing because I knew the tests could hurt my baby in the womb.

Finally, I agreed when one doctor told me the test might give me an indication of how severe my baby's Down syndrome would be. And that knowledge might help me better prepare for life with him.

I went to another doctor to schedule the test, and he said, "We need to do this right away because you're so close to the legal cut-off date for termination."

I said, "I'm not worried about that. I just want to determine the potential severity of the Down syndrome."

He furrowed his brow and said, "This test only gives you a positive or negative. It doesn't predict the severity."

I walked out.

Everybody wanted me to terminate. Nobody wanted to help me prepare for my baby's arrival.

I found out later from the Down syndrome community that there is literature out there to help you prepare. But doctors don't allow it in their offices because it might convince women to keep their children.

When Noah was born, his condition was a lot worse than I had expected. He was born with a blocked bowel and needed an operation, and he had a hole in his heart that would require another surgery. He also had something called hydrops fetalis, which is not specific to Down syndrome, but has a mortality rate of 90%! Doctors just don't know how to fix it. All you can do is hope for the best.

They told me, "Look, Jackie, hydrops plus Down Syndrome is just not survivable. He won't make it a month.

You need to prepare for his death. Do you have a relative or friend who can come in and be with you? Maybe take some video or pictures of you with the baby in your arms before he dies?"

I said no.

And then I spent the next several months researching and getting into fights with doctors. All of them wanted me to give up. To let Noah die. I lost track of how many doctors pulled me aside and advised me to "let it go."

By the way, this whole time I was also running a restaurant! I had a team of people holding down the fort while I was away, but there was still plenty for me to do virtually from our hospital room.

Google Plus—and More

I spent a lot of time on Google during those months. There was this new platform called Google Plus, and I was all over it.

I have an IT background, so I'm often an "early adopter." I had been messing about with Plus and Hangouts and was checking out all these tools to see if I could connect with other food bloggers and influencers. I'd jump on, hang out with these folks and talk about podcasts and blogs.

Google was about to introduce another tool called Hangouts On-Air. They saw all my activity on Google Plus and contacted me about the new widget. "Hey, Jackie. We would love to talk to you about Google Hangouts On-Air and how you can use it for your business."

I received that email while Noah was resting next to me in the hospital bed. I thought, "Oh my God, all I need is one more thing to think about!" I was barely holding myself together.

But, I replied, "OK. I just want to let you know that I've just given birth. But let's hop on a call. Give me a few days."

On the call, a Google rep told me they wanted me to do a cooking session "on air" so people halfway around the world could tune in, watch me cook, ask questions and even cook along with me. They called it a "Cook-Along."

Well, "Cook-Along" never worked out with Google, but the idea prompted me to start a virtual cooking show on my own. I'd do one or two shows a week even as I continued to go to the hospital every day to see Noah and run the restaurant.

When Noah was three months old, doctors told me he needed a second heart surgery. But they didn't want to do it. Essentially, they said, "If we don't do it, he might die. If we do it, his condition is so weak, we're going to have to hook him up to a heart–lung machine. If we do that, at his age, he's going to get brain damage, and he's going to be a vegetable for the rest of his life. So, I suggest we don't treat him. We let him die. You're not getting any younger, Jackie, and who's going to look after him when you're gone? He's going to be a burden on society."

I said, "If those are my only options—to let him die or do the surgery—then I say: Do the surgery."

God is in control.

One doctor got really upset with me. Then he turned and rolled his eyes at the heart surgeon, like "She's crazy." The heart surgeon said, "Sorry, my team and I are not going to play executioner to this baby."

I said, "Then you're going to let him die?"

He got really mad because I had called his bluff. He admitted there *was* a third option: Hold off on the surgery for a bit.

I nodded.

"Fine!" he sputtered. "In that case, I'm going to put in the paperwork to have your son transferred out of the neonatal ICU. He's three months now and is technically not neonatal anymore. Secondly, we've run out of ideas on what to do with him. Third, we need the bed back."

They kicked Noah out of the neonatal ICU because the doctors didn't think he was worth saving.

New Ideas

They moved Noah into a pediatric ICU, which turned out to be a blessing in disguise. The move brought in a completely new team of specialists to oversee his progress. These doctors had different ideas: ideas about how to keep him alive instead of how to let him die.

Noah improved dramatically under their care. Within a couple months, he was strong enough for the heart surgery.

Unfortunately, things were *not* improving at the restaurant, and we were getting bad reviews. "Staff is rude." "Food is overrated." I thought about making big changes, firing a bunch of folks, disputing the bad reviews. Stirring up fires.

Instead, I went back to those four words. God is in control.

And when I meditated on those words, I began thinking about leaving the restaurant entirely. I didn't know how I could do that if I didn't have another source of income. I just knew God was in control.

I wrote a blog post addressing the bad reviews and publicity. It said something like:

> I've been dealing with a very sick child for a number of months and I haven't been able to manage the restaurant the way I'd like. But never mind that. If you feel you've been ripped off by my restaurant, I'll give you your money back. Also, from now on, if I can't be at the restaurant, we just won't open that day. If I have an emergency with Noah, I just won't open. That's how much I value giving great service.

I didn't know how I would keep a restaurant thriving if I had to shut it down every time I couldn't make it in! But God was in control.

The day after I published that blog post, two guys I had never met walked into my restaurant. They said, "Hey, we are interested in buying your space. How much would you take for it?"

I sold my restaurant that day and walked out of it with a big check in my pocket!

God is in control.

Noah had the surgery and survived. And, one week before Christmas, after 217 days in the hospital, he finally came home.

Growing an Audience

After about six months of not checking Google Plus, I logged in and discovered I had tens of thousands of followers!

Google must have been promoting my profile on this new platform because it considered me someone who created interesting content. God was in control—even while I was sleeping!

Over the next couple of years, I built my following on Google Plus to 1.86 million. I was the Number One Most Followed Australian on Google Plus.

Of course, when Google Plus shut down in 2019, I lost 1.86 million followers, but it's remarkable what that size audience can do for your notoriety even over just a few years!

Being known as one of the most influential people in social media has opened thousands of doors for me. Free computers. Free travel. Television appearances. Podcast interviews. Lots and lots of little blessings.

But most of all: freedom.

And I used that freedom to create my online cooking course, which now allows me to completely focus my efforts online.

Which allows me to spend more time with Noah.

Sometimes we try really hard to look for signs, symbols and cryptic messages. We put too much reliance on spiritual people who "hear" from realms we can't hear from. Sometimes we put too much emphasis on churches, temples and altars.

Sometimes it's better to just keep going back to words that got imprinted on our hearts, for whatever reason, years or even decades ago.

Those are *our* words.

Those are *your* words.

Write them on your heart, so you hear them every time it beats!

Pick up your bonus material and all the appendices free at www.perrymarshall.com/morememos.

Chapter 10

INSIDE THE POPCORN POPPER

From Genet Jones, a copywriter, editor and book coach who lives in Bentonville, Arkansas.

I was looking for direction after bouncing around from career to career for about a decade. I had a computer science degree and a real estate license. I had worked as a website designer and been certified as a health coach.

I had tried all these things, but none of them felt like my "vocation" or "calling" or "purpose." I would get enthusiastic about something for a while, but then it would just trail off.

I just didn't know what I was meant to do.

At the time of my memo, I thought I was supposed to be a health coach and had invested a lot of time and money into this idea. But the field was quickly becoming saturated, and I was by no means confident in this decision.

Then came Perry's invitation to a "Memos from the Head Office" session.

I had been in Perry's world for about a year. A friend of mine had started a business, and her husband, who was a type of serial entrepreneur, followed Perry. Because I was doing some content writing for them, he recommended I follow Perry too.

Over the next year or so, I got deeper and deeper into Perry's world and eventually joined his "30-Day Reboot" program, which offered a "Memos from the Head Office" call. I didn't initially want to join the call and was almost ashamed of myself when I did. I did not think any of this memos stuff actually happened, and I suspected people who promoted that kind of thing were shysters.

So, I really surprised myself when I joined that call. I think the main reason I chose to participate was that it did not seem like persuasion, hype or a "pitch," and also because I really wanted some direction. So, both those things overrode my skepticism.

Deep inside, I thought: "It doesn't really matter whether you believe in this stuff or not. You need to have a look. If you can get some direction from this, fine. If not, you have nothing to lose by listening."

I was at a low point in my self-confidence, in my spirituality, in a lot of things.

When I was younger, I sought out spiritual things and was what I'd call a "spiritual kid." For example, I had been really great at finding things that were lost. I had this ability to "tune in" to where that object would be. It's hard to explain, but I was very intuitive, and it worked.

But I'd had some bad experiences with organized religion, which seemed more interested in rules and regulations than what I would call "spirituality." I didn't realize then that I could seek spiritual things outside of the religious system. So, I denied my intuition and threw all of it out.

Eventually, I came to believe, "If you can't measure it, then it doesn't exist."

But that mindset can lead to a big void in your life. I was feeling the void.

Go Ahead, Get Creative

The memos people were working only from a list of names. None of us even spoke to them on the call, and no one had submitted questions or anything like that.

When Julie got to my name, she said, "I see you inside a popcorn popper, always bouncing from one thing to another. It's time to settle on one thing, but you still need to explore what that is."

Then Gary said, "And this is something creative. It will draw on your creativity. Not necessarily the arts, but something creative."

My reaction?

Well, the "popcorn popper" comment gave me shivers down my spine. "Yes, that's exactly what I've been doing. How did she know that?"

And the creative comment? Well, that made me pause. I had started writing stories when I was 8 years old and had always been good with words. In fact, I thought about getting a journalism or English degree when I entered college but thought that path seemed too easy!

I thought then that if you didn't have to work really hard at something, then it wasn't worth doing. And because English courses—working with words, being creative—came naturally to me, then it could not be worth pursuing. Plus, our culture says you can't make a living as a "creative." Who wants to be a starving artist?

So, I got a computer science degree instead. I distinctly remember as I was getting deep into that field, having dreams about going through my life as if it were a program. It totally shifted the way my brain naturally worked. Remember how I said, "If you can't measure it, it doesn't exist?" That's how far I shifted my brain to the other side!

I had suppressed my creative side so much that I almost forgot I had one! Yeah, I know. Perry calls that "head trash." I had a noggin full.

These memos were dead-on accurate and sent chills down my back. So, I stuffed them under a pile of papers on my desk and ignored them. "I've spent too much time and money on this health coach stuff. I need to pursue it. I'm throwing myself into completing my certification and building that business, doggone it!"

You can probably guess what happened. My health coaching business went nowhere fast. And while I was sprinting in place on that job, three people approached me to do website copy work—which I had not done in 10 years!

What was going on? The thing that I thought I should do wasn't working *at all*. The only offers were for something creative I did 10 years ago!

So frustrating.

One day, I was headed to a networking event. I had done enough of these to know that people who try to promote more than one business at these events never do a good job of promoting either one. I knew I had to make a choice between health coach or wordsmith.

I remember talking with a friend about it. "Which direction do you think I should go?" She advised me to think about my "innate talents."

And that's when I remembered the memo. I dug it out from under the stack of papers on my desk and read it again.

And I thought, "My gift is words. I need to go back to that."

That memo gave me the confidence to say, "OK, I put all this effort into being a health coach, but maybe I need to follow my true self instead."

So, I went to that networking meeting and promoted myself as a writer and editor. Not a health coach.

At the meeting, a woman came up to me and asked, "Do you sub-contract?"

I said, "Well, yes."

And I have had at least one contract with that creative agency ever since! Nearly three years now.

Fast forward three years from that memos call, and I'm writing web content for a creative agency and several web designers. I'm working with two authors as their developmental editor or coauthor. I'm working through *The Artist's Way*. And I'm having a massive spiritual reawakening. I have more space, more peace, more balance in my life.

I'm back in touch with my creative and intuitive side. I've regained my comfort and enthusiasm for tuning in to the universe to "find things" I need. And more of the best kinds of clients without sacrificing my personal life.

That financial improvement has been really fortunate for me because I'm a homeschooling mom. I can't work full time—and now I don't have to!

I think there's probably still some financial head trash I need to work on. But there has been steady improvement.

MORE THAN ONE CHANNEL

Perry here. Not all memos stories are "unmistakable connecting of dots" like the day Vivian told me I was working on a math problem. Many memos stories could be dismissed by others as some random person saying some random thing and us poor suckers wanting to connect the dots so bad, we just do it however we want.

And maybe that's how it looks from the outside. What's harder to see, however, is that often when we're getting a memo through the A channel (our ears), the Head Office is speaking to us at the very same time through the B channel (our hearts).

I think this is what was happening in Genet's story. It happens to me a lot, and not even necessarily in a "memos environment." I might be at a conference, speaking to a client or talking on the phone. While someone is speaking to me through the A channel, my B channel starts whispering. Then I get out my little notebook and start writing stuff down, so I don't miss anything. It happens most often when I'm in a state of "flow."

That is exactly what happened to me the day I got the calculus formula for the 80/20 Curve, the one now published in *Harvard Business Review Italia*. I was leading a Roundtable meeting, so I was supposed to be paying very close attention as I was the consultant and they were the clients.

Someone was presenting. Members were bantering back and forth with questions and discussion. I was sitting there with my yellow pad of paper sketching out this 80/20 problem for probably the 20th time, when suddenly I could see how to work it out.

It fell together so elegantly. It was easy. "Why didn't I see this before?" I went home, hired a math guy on the web to solve an integral element for me, and the job was done. Just like that. That was three years after I got the memo from Vivian.

There's a story in Appendix 2 (at www.perrymarshall.com/morememos) about Isabel Allum "reading me my mail" for 12 minutes. From the outside, her comments might not look all that insightful and certainly not like "insider knowledge." But her words were releasing a stream of images inside my head and igniting sparks in my heart. The sheer resonance of that experience was overwhelming, and 15 years later I still remember it vividly.

Sometimes in group memo sessions, a speaker might say something like, "If someone else gets a memo and something jumps out that you like, grab onto it because you can have it too." That doesn't mean the whole event is a big giant candy store and anyone can take any memo they want.

Instead it means, if you're hearing someone else's memo through the A channel, and the Head Office speaks to you through the B channel and says grab onto that, then by all means, grab onto it. You may need to sit with it awhile. You may process it further or ask for more insight later. It may mean something entirely different for you than it meant for the other person. But it's raw material to create a new movement for you in your life.

THE HOLY SPIRIT HIGHLIGHTER

Once in a while when I'm reading Scriptures, a verse or paragraph will leap off the page, leaving no question that I need to sit up and pay very close attention. I call this the "Holy Spirit Highlighter," and here are two examples of how that tool has worked in my life.

Light Will Dispel the Darkness

In 2009, we were two years into attempting to organize our first adoption, which was fraught with problems, such as our agency going out of business and having to start over. I was completely overwhelmed with business challenges, family problems, the shaky economy at the time (remember the crash?). Plus, we already had four kids of our own, and I was also on the tail end of a messy personal crisis. I thought, "How are we possibly going to add one more kid to the careening jalopy of our life without sending our whole family sailing over a cliff in billowing flames and smoke?"

I couldn't imagine how I was going to make it all work. One afternoon, I was reading Isaiah, which says:

Is this really the kind of fasting I want?

Do I want a day when people merely humble themselves,
bowing their heads like a reed
and stretching out on sackcloth and ashes?
Is this really what you call a fast, a day that is pleasing to
the Lord?

No, this is the kind of fast I want:
I want you to remove the sinful chains,
to tear away the ropes of the burdensome yoke,
to set free the oppressed and to break every burdensome
yoke.

I want you to share your food with the hungry
and to provide shelter for homeless, oppressed people.
When you see someone naked, clothe them!
Don't turn your back on your own flesh and blood.

Then your light will shine like the sunrise;
your restoration will quickly arrive;
your godly behavior will go before you, and the Lord's
splendor will be your rear guard.

Then you will call out, and the Lord will respond;
you will cry out, and he will reply, 'Here I am.'
You must remove the burdensome yoke from among you
and stop pointing fingers and speaking sinfully.

You must actively help the hungry
and feed the oppressed.
Then your light will dispel the darkness,
and your darkness will be transformed into noonday.[4]

---

4 Isa. 58:5-10 NET

When I say these words "leaped off the page at me," I mean leaped. Those words attacked me like a barking dog. The message was unmistakable: "Perry, when you take care of the people I care about, I take care of you."

I let the anxiety slide off and said: "OK. If that's what you want us to do, then that's what we'll do. From now on, I'll put one foot in front of the other, and I'm not gonna worry about how it's all going to fall together."

Two years later, we adopted a 19-month-old girl from China. I'm not going to pretend for a second that it was all rose petals and martinis at the beach. It wasn't. But it did work out, and we wouldn't trade our daughter for the world. And our family did not sail over a cliff in flames and smoke.

Strong, Like an Iron Pillar

In 2005, about a year after what is now known as my Evolution 2.0 project began, I was working to pound the slag off of my most important ideas, and those ideas were making some people mad, even though my conversations were with either small groups of people or one-on-one. Evolution 2.0 is an effort to understand where life came from on Planet Earth. It's about the "big questions."

One day I was emailing back and forth with a guy and wound up backing him into a corner. He wasn't liking it very much, so he went to the world's largest atheist website, which at the time was called Internet Infidels (infidels.org). He logged onto their massive discussion board and posted a link to a somewhat famous talk I'd given called, "If You Can Read This, I Can Prove God Exists."

Suddenly, I was on a world stage being forced to defend myself.

There was one of me and at least 50 of them. I knew if I made even the tiniest slip or mistake, they would eviscerate me like a pack of ravenous wolves. I thought, "*Oh no*—I really did not want this. Not now, and especially not with these people!"

I was *scared*. As in, obsess 24/7 and lie awake all night long scared. As in, go back every two hours, argue some more, dot every "i" and cross every "t" scared.

Let me give you a better appreciation of how alarming this was. This was 2005. In 2003, I had written my book about Google ads. At the time, Google was just an eccentric "dot com" that most people had never heard of. But 2003 was the year their advertising system took off, and by 2005 Google was beginning to take over the world. This was turning into a magic carpet ride for me, and Vivian's prophecy was suddenly coming true.

I was the hot new kid on the internet marketing scene, and my books were selling like hotcakes. Speaking invitations were pouring in from Cleveland to Australia. I had a sterling reputation. If you typed "Perry Marshall" into Google, you found nothing but glowing reviews. At least in my tiny little corner of the internet, everybody loved Perry.

But now, I felt l like I had moved into a gorgeous brand-new house with lovely flowers and a picket fence in the front yard—and my kitchen was engulfed in flames. The fire in the kitchen was this fight on Infidels, as I shall soon describe in more detail. The stove was burning. Smoke was billowing out the windows. It was threatening to burn my house down. I was terrified this was going to destroy my business and reputation, because these guys were *mad*. And there were a lot of them. This became a giant anxiety machine.

A few days later, I was reading the first chapter of Jeremiah and suddenly these words *leaped* off the page:

Get up. Get dressed. Go out and tell them whatever
I tell you to say. Do not be afraid of them or I will make
you a fool before their eyes.

For see, today I have made you immune to their
attacks. You are strong, like an iron pillar or brass wall,
a fortified city that cannot be taken. None of the kings,
priests, officials or people of Judah will be able to stand
against you. They will try and they will fail. I am with you
and I will take care of you. I, the Lord, have spoken![5]

Like I said, it just leaped off the page. Unmistakable.

So, I mopped the perspiration from my brow and
memorized every word. I remember taking breaks during
my workday, going outside, walking around the block and
reciting these words to myself. Over and over. Doing my
best to quell the incessant chattering in my brain.

What happened next?

Like I said, there was one of me and 50 of them. As
several weeks went by, even more opponents showed up,
which I thought put me at a severe disadvantage.

I strictly limited myself to posting once a week, every
week, then logging out and not even peeking at the replies
until the following week, when it was time to do it all over
again. That was the only way I could keep the obsession and
anxiety from ripping me to shreds. These debates could not
be allowed to distract me from running my business.

Once each week, late at night, I would spend about
three hours responding to the folks on Infidels, asserting
my position and insisting that they come forward with
evidence. My shoulders and neck muscles were always in
knots by the time I got to bed. Soon the fury of Infidels
started spilling out on literally more than 1,000 websites. If
you typed "Perry Marshall idiot" into Google, you would

---

5 Jer. 1:17-19

find page after page of people declaring how stupid I was.

The science conversations were attracting more traffic than my business, and I knew if I made one mistake, one slip, one tiny error, these guys would rip me to shreds and destroy my reputation. They belonged to a crowd that had destroyed many other careers over this exact issue.

At the time, I did not have the arguments all worked out like I do now. I was pretty sure I was right, but I worried that there was a big gaping hole in my knowledge. I was barely managing to stay one step ahead of the wolf pack.

But as it turns out, being severely outnumbered gave me the upper hand because I placed the burden of proof on them. I demanded they provide evidence to support their position. "Show me a code that's not designed," I insisted.

They had no evidence. Just stories. And they couldn't get their stories straight. None of them could even agree on how to respond. I had a simple, straightforward, unwavering thesis. Their position was a cacophony of conflicting views, which only made them angrier. At no point were they ever able to counter my evidence, which was that DNA is digital code (like 1s and 0s in computers), and nobody knows how to get a code without designing one. The mystery of where life came from has never been solved.

This became the longest-running, most-viewed thread in the history of the world's largest atheist discussion board. The thread continued for seven years. It picked up over 100,000 page views. Every time a new post appeared in the forum, it shot the whole thing straight to the top of the directory. My case was robust, so I even started buying ads on Google and driving traffic to it, to make it clear who really had the upper hand.

A few years later, a radio host heard my story and invited me to come on his program. He wanted to match me with a skeptic so we could debate this on the air, head to head. His extensive network included some of the most famous atheists in the world, but he reached out a few days before our interview and said, "Perry, I've combed through my entire contact database. I cannot find a single person who is willing to debate you." He had to cancel my appearance and go with a different topic.[6]

Remember that verse in Jeremiah? "None of the kings, priests, officials or people of Judah will be able to stand against you. They will try, and they will fail."

LISTENING WITH CONFIDENCE

I cannot tell you how much confidence you wield when you know the Head Office is backing you. My friend, if it takes you 10 years and untold miles of unpaved roads to gain that confidence, it's worth it. Because remember: 10 years from now, whether you've cultivated your connection with heaven or not, either way you're still gonna be 10 years older.

Eventually, I got tired of arguing with people, and the time came to stop having philosophical debates with folks who didn't want to listen anyway. I decided to cast that chip off my shoulder and transform this project into something far larger, something much more useful for science and humanity.

So, after my book *Evolution 2.0* was published in 2015, I announced a $10 million prize by the same name. It is an award for discovering the origin of genetics and life on earth. Complete details of this story are told in Chapters 24 and 25 of my book, *Evolution 2.0*.

It's the exact same problem I was presenting on Infidels, but instead of slinging missives back and forth on some discussion board, we're offering money for a solution. Sort of like the X-Prize for space flight. As I'm writing this in 2021, it's the world's largest basic science research award, almost 10 times bigger than the Nobel.

---

6 I have since debated some skeptics, including PZ Myers. See https://evo2.org/pz-myers/.

I could not have imagined my dive into the swamp of Internet Infidels would someday bring me to the doorstep of the Royal Society of Great Britain; press coverage in *The Financial Times*, *Voices from Oxford*, and numerous peer-reviewed science journals; or chairing sessions at a cancer symposium. Favor from the Head Office can transport you to remarkable places.

This is why cultivating your listening ear is the ultimate $10,000 an hour skill.

Chapter 11

SCREAMING OBSCENITIES AT GOD ON THE 405

From Bonnie Kim, a consultant who lives in Los Angeles, California.

I was consulting in the tech industry for a guy named Jason. At the beginning, our project was all optimism, unicorns and rainbows.

But our relationship quickly deteriorated. Jason got tightfisted. He started pinching nickels and shaving pennies, asking me to do more but refusing to pay more. Chiseling me.

This baffled me because we had both been very clear about what was needed and what expenditures would be before we started our project. All spelled out in the contract. But something changed with Jason. I'm not sure why.

Several times I caught him doing end runs around

me, trying to get my employees to do something I had not authorized, and he had not paid for!

For several weeks, we were sharp pebbles in each other's shoes. One of the most irritating relationships I've ever endured. Garden-rake-on-blackboard irritating.

Eventually, he told me, "We need to cut ties. This is a toxic client-consultant relationship. It's not good for either of us anymore."

Fine with me.

Just one catch: He wanted a refund of everything he'd paid!

Technically, he broke the contract—and he wanted a refund! He had gone behind my back but wanted his money back. He had gotten tightfisted, not acted in good faith. And he was asking for a refund!

I don't think I've ever been angrier in my life. My rage needle was buried in the red.

So, one day I'm driving down the San Diego Expressway—better known as the 405—screeching at God, "This is so unfair! Why is he doing this to me?"

That's when I got the memo.

"Forgive him."

I literally shrieked in the car, "*Noooooooo!*"

If anyone saw me, they surely thought I was a nut job. I can just imagine some commuter calling 911 and telling the operator, "Some Asian psycho chick in a gray Acura is driving southbound on the 405, screaming and shaking her fist at her sunroof."

I said, "Forgive him? You gotta be flippin' kidding me. It's his fault!"

Then I heard, "Bless your enemies."

The only word I can think of to describe the feeling that washed over me at that moment is "convicted." Sometimes the Head Office nails ya.

I realized, I'm not "supposed" to behave this way.

Even though he *is* wrong. Even though I am justified. Even though I am the victim. It's my job to forgive. It's my job to bring peace.

So, I said aloud right there in the car, "I forgive Jason."

I decided in my heart I would not hold any curses or negative thoughts toward Jason from that point on. I resolved to let him go.

Not more than five minutes later, I got a text from an old friend I had not heard from in over a decade, "I have a friend who needs you."

His friend used to be an organizer at the World Economic Forum.

A few days later, I spoke on the phone with this gentleman. And he hired me. The engagement we agreed upon was 400% more than my engagement with Jason. I have been serving that same client for over three years, and he has never asked for a refund.

That's right—five minutes after I received my memo and acted on it, I got back what was "stolen" from me. Many times over.

I even got to meet with Jason one last time. I asked for forgiveness in person. I said, "I take ownership for any way I might have disrespected you or hurt you. I'm sorry for that and hope you'll forgive me."

It was a peaceful meeting. The irritation and suspicion all washed away. I was even comfortable enough to suggest to Jason that he might want to seek counseling and healing about his "financial head trash." He accepted the advice with an open mind and generous spirit.

Perry here. I would like to offer some observations based on Bonnie's story because it offers several key points about how you can get more memos.

Don't Forget to Ask

First, if you want more memos, you have to ask! That might seem like a strange observation based on Bonnie's story. When in this story did Bonnie ask for a memo?

When she was screaming at God in her car.

Wait. "Screaming is asking?"

My answer: If it is honest and heartfelt, then yes, screaming is asking.

Do you think the Head Office is more scared of your emotions than you are? This is another misunderstood aspect about memos: You don't have to ask nicely. Providence does not care whether you ask nicely. Providence just wants you to ask. Heaven would much rather you scream and complain than remain silent.

It's about relationship. Not rules.

In the Hebrew Bible, there's a famous guy named King David. God called David, "a man after my own heart." David's Higher Power even made David king, and David wrote a bunch of songs to his Higher Power. They're called psalms.

And in those psalms, David does a lot of "crying out" to God, and he frequently is not polite! He takes the gloves off. Lets God know exactly how he feels. Sometimes it's downright shocking. Cringeworthy even.

At some point or another, most of the prophets in the Hebrew Bible tell God in no uncertain terms "Dude, if you treated us better, you might have more friends."

Is it really OK to talk to God that way?

Well, God calls David a "man after my own heart." Why? Because David was honest.

When I read David's psalms as a kid, I noticed that in one chapter, he'd be soaring above the clouds, and the next chapter, he'd be dredging a radioactive emotional sewage canal. I would think to myself "David. David. What's the matter with you, you manic depressive pile of goo?"

I related much more easily to Solomon's proverbs. Wise, useful, practical stuff. Brain stuff, not heart stuff.

Once my college English prof (wonderful, insightful guy) asked our class, "Which of you always knows how you feel?"

It was the sort of question you're not supposed to answer affirmatively. But I didn't catch his drift, and I said yes. I was the only one.

He politely ignored it, but I'm sure he thought "Perry doesn't even know he doesn't know how he feels on any given day." Back then, I mostly lived in my head.

A few years ago, a counselor said to me, "You know what Perry? You are *really* good at hiding your shit." (Considering the starchy church culture I grew up in, this was actually quite a compliment.)

She was right. I was so good, I was even hiding it from myself. But push eventually came to shove, and I had to figure out why I was so compulsive. And why certain things would drive me into a rage. Why I would snap at people and seemingly have no control of myself. Why certain things my kids did pushed my buttons so hard. Why there were some events I could barely even talk about.

At one point, my toothpaste started belching out of the tube, and I just couldn't shove it back anymore.

When you're 20, you have the strength to keep it all smoothed over. When you're 40, you need some of that energy for other things. Very old wounds started coming to the surface.

Little by little, I began to see that underneath my well-orchestrated exterior was a hurting boy, an aching young man—a kid who didn't know what to do with those hurts, so he buried them.

That's when I began to understand David and his poetic, emotional roller coaster.

David always kept lines of communication open. Even when he was pissed. Even when he was not on God's "good side." He kept talking. He kept crying out.

That's what Bonnie did. She didn't strap herself into a straitjacket and declare "Before I ask for a memo, I must calm my mind, read soothing and worshipful homilies, then when I feel that I'm acceptable to The Almighty, I will approach with reverence, respect and timidity—and *then* I will humbly beseech his help."

No, she started yelling and screaming. From the depths of her spitting, outraged heart.

"Out of the depths I cry to you, oh Lord! Oh Lord, hear my voice!" Like David did in Psalm 130.

If you want to hear more memos—ask. Do not worry about how you ask or whether you're asking the "correct" way. Don't worry that the Architect of the universe will be offended and freeze you out.

The Source wants a relationship with you. If that relationship is shouting and anger, the Higher Power prefers that to silence or rote, empty prayers and genuflections. Or manners and politeness. Messy is OK.

Just belt it out.

FOLLOW THE MEMO!

The next step in getting more memos is to *do* what it says! Do the thing. Follow the advice. Implement the strategy. Make the phone call. Send the email.

Yeah. I know you're almost never 147% sure it was a *real* memo and not just last night's jalapeños. Believe me, I know there's always that margin of uncertainty.

So, if it's a big ask or major change in direction, you should ask again and again. Seek more confirmation until you're sure. Remember, there's no iron law that says you have to take action immediately.

But when you follow the memo, you prove that you're listening to the Head Office. And when you prove that you're listening, you'll get more memos. And the memos will become clearer, so you won't continue to confuse them with the effects of a spicy meal.

THE MOST POWERFUL FORCE IN THE UNIVERSE?

Most important, to hear more memos, tap into the most powerful way of opening up the channels of communication: forgiveness.

Trying to hear memos when your heart is roiling with resentment and anger is like trying to pick up a signal on a 1980s TV set with no antenna. The memos haven't stopped coming; they are still streaming through the airwaves. But your ability to see, hear and recognize them gets choked off.

As you forgive, something wonderful and magical happens. The Muse tilts toward you and places its lips to your ear. What was once a murmur becomes a trumpet blast. What was once a screen of static and snow becomes a 72-inch, 4K, high-definition flat screen. (Well, sometimes anyway.)

I'm not sure why it works this way, but I can offer some educated guesses. When you do not forgive, you are essentially saying "I actually like clinging to this hurt, this pain, this trauma, this insult."

Your heart has been damaged, and all it knows how to do is clench. It feels so unfair, vulnerable and even dangerous to let go of those feelings. It's one of the most difficult things we humans do.

But if you can summon the courage to let it go, to say "I forgive you, I release you, you owe me nothing"—and really mean it—then you're free. Your heart unclenches. (By the way, you don't even have to "want" to forgive. It's good enough to want to want to forgive.)

When your heart unclenches, it opens. And becomes ready to receive more memos.

And just like in Bonnie's story, miracles happen very soon after you clear this channel.

"Answer the Phone; It's Good News!"

I (Perry) occasionally hold two-day consulting sessions in my home. During one of these, on August 1, 2013, the very first day, a CEO mentioned he was in the middle of a bogus lawsuit. But when I tried to get him to tell us about it, he muttered, "I really don't want to talk about that right now," and so we moved on.

The next morning, I woke up early for my Renaissance time, as I always do to journal and listen for memos. When I journal, I pray, I ask questions and I write down *whatever* answer seems to be coming back to me. Even if it seems to make no sense at all—I still write it down.

At 6:30 that morning I said, "OK, what do you want me to talk about today during the meeting?"

And this what I "heard": "Ask that guy about his lawsuit. And talk to him about inner healing."

I made a note of that.

A couple of hours later, everybody showed up for the day's session. As we were finishing our coffee and pastries, just about ready to get rolling, I turned to the CEO and said, "Oh, I'm supposed to ask you about your lawsuit. Tell me about your lawsuit."

So, he told me about his lawsuit. I looked at my watch: 9:20 a.m. Then I told him that during inner healing sessions, when I'm trying to clear out my "head trash," I often end up forgiving somebody who did something to me.

"When you forgive the person, your heart opens you up, and you can receive better. It's very often a major part of a turnaround," I went on. "This person is suing you, and they're crazy, and I know you want to strangle them, but I want to ask something of you."

The CEO and his wife both nodded and asked me to go on.

I said, "This is totally counterintuitive, but I'm asking you to forgive this person in your heart. Even though this person is trying to strangle you and get money out of you, I want you to ask God to bless this person and give this person good things in their life."

They both looked at me, then at each other, then back at me. "OK. All right, I get that. Yeah, we could do that."

Just then his phone buzzed in his pocket. It was 9:24

a.m. Exactly 4 minutes after I started telling the CEO about the power of forgiveness. He pulled out the phone and said, "It's my attorney. He wants me to call him."

I said, "It's good news!"

His wife said, "It's *never* good news when that guy calls!"

I volleyed back, "It's good news! Go take the call!"

The CEO left the room. He came back 10 minutes later and announced, "They want to settle, and they are willing to settle for $10,000 less than I decided I would take last week."

A couple weeks later, he wrote a settlement check for $120,000. It was all done.

Now, I want us to stop and consider what happened in this story. I prayed, "Tell me what to talk about." I got an answer.

I mentioned the concept of forgiveness at 9:20 a.m. We finished our conversation at 9:24 when he agreed to forgive the person. His phone buzzed in his pocket at that moment.

Before the CEO could get that text message, the woman suing him had to talk to her attorney.

And then her attorney had to talk to my client's attorney.

And then my client's attorney had to text my client.

And that whole chain of events culminated *exactly* when our conversation about forgiveness ended. Now remember, this lawsuit had been dragging on for two years, hanging over his head like the sword of Damocles. By my reckoning, the chances of that text message coming at 9:24 by sheer coincidence are about one in 5,000.

It's trippy. I have a very hard time believing it was coincidence. If you want to ascribe this event to chance, then I can't stop you from doing so. You can decide to believe that if you want. But I say, if you're gonna chalk up all the stories in this book to chance, then you're engaging in statistics abuse.

FORGIVENESS IS TIME TRAVEL

Forgiveness fixes problems that already happened—in reverse.

In my experience, the universe is far stranger than any scientific theorem. And forgiveness is much *better* than normal human logic and "justice."

Justice would have boxed Bonnie Kim into a fit of rage and anger. Forgiveness opened up the lines of communication.

Forgiveness cancels psychic debt. Debt that sludges up every department of your life.

So, if you really want to receive more memos, then start by asking yourself "Who do I need to forgive?"

Write down their names. *Right now.* In the little box on the next page, write, "I forgive _____."

It might be a long process. Might be very painful. It might take all the courage you possess. But there's nothing more urgent.

Start. Not tomorrow—today.

I forgive:

1.

2.

3.

4.

5.

Don't forget to claim your bonus material with additional stories
and videos, and all the appendices at
www.perrymarshall.com/morememos.

Chapter 12

SEATBELT WARNING AT 134TH AND EAST ELM ROAD

From Jason Pieratt who is a vice president of operations for Children's Relief International, a charitable organization headquartered in Rockwall, Texas.

I spent most of my high school summers in rural Nebraska. I loved driving the backroads from the village of Filley to the big town of Beatrice. It has a Walmart!

When time allowed, I'd take my favorite route: 134th to East Elm Road. It wasn't the fastest route, but 134th is blacktop and has a fun, sharp bend and a nice stretch that will cause "blacktop butterflies" when you hit it at the right speed. At Elm Road, the blacktop turns to gravel and the hills get a bit steeper. Four miles down sits the grand Zion Lutheran Church.

In 1997, I drove this route *a lot*. One particular drive stands out.

I had the windows down, cranking some Soundgarden at full volume. I hit 134th at the perfect speed for blacktop butterflies. As I slowed to turn on to East Elm, I felt a voice. It wasn't audible, and it was more than a voice, it was a "voice–feeling."

"Put your seatbelt on."

I didn't wear my seatbelt much in those days. Certainly not on the back roads. Yet "Put your seatbelt on" felt strong enough that I clicked in.

Less than two miles down, I met another car at the top of one of the rolling hills. I remember a panicked swerve.

And then . . . black.

I woke up upside down in a deep ditch. I couldn't unbuckle. Everything hurt. I tried to move but couldn't.

And then . . . black again.

My next memory is shuffling down the middle of Elm Road toward a farmhouse.

How did I get out of my demolished car? I still don't know. But months and years later, little flickers of memory would return.

I saw something bright. And that "something bright" helped me through the window.

I don't know what it was. Angel? Jesus? God? Holy Spirit? All I know is that it was very bright.

I was saved by a firm voice and a bright helper.

Plus the seatbelt!

One thing is 100% certain. If I had not been wearing my seatbelt, I would have died that day. Period.

Something saw me headed in the wrong direction. Something called out to me. Something saved me.

I didn't ask for it. I wasn't asking for directions. I wasn't thinking "What should I be doing next?" Nothing like that.

I wasn't praying. In fact, I was lost in the pure adrenaline pleasure of the moment. The speed, the beautiful rolling hills, the screaming hard rock music.

I was caught up in my fun and joy. And God gently but firmly butted in and saved me to live another day.

Over the summer of 2019, I felt a bit like my missionary staff and our supporters were cruising down 134th and Elm, enjoying the bend and blacktop butterflies. It was all smiles and laughs as we took in the cool air and the dips and the grand view of his Zion Church. We were buckled up, and the ride was good!

And yet in the midst of the good, I thought I heard the same firm voice. It felt very much like the firm, soft voice I had heard years ago. God was providing direction and maybe a warning again. And I believed it was something I was supposed to share with my tribe.

"There are so many more who need help."
"Stay focused."
"Stay true."

This was the 2019 version of "put your seatbelt on." And the message wasn't just for me but for my whole tribe, so I shared it with them. And then I said:

We can't predict what that future will hold for us as CRI relief workers, but this "word" gives us a renewed sense of focus and resolve.

Stay focused.

Stay true.

Today, more than ever, we are trusting that God will continue to guide us, despite any distractions and in the midst of our thanksgiving and hope. We are trusting that he will do the same in the lives of our friends and supporters. Because we need them, the very best of them, this day and in the days to come.

I don't know if listening to that word helped us avoid a "crash." I don't know if we narrowly skidded out of the way of some disastrous impact.

As I write this in early 2021, we've had our share of upsets, but no crashes. No disasters.

Maybe someday in the future, we'll be able to look back and say, "We nearly skidded off the road there, but because we had our seatbelt on, we survived to help hundreds of more poor kids."

I don't know. You can't prove a negative.

But here's what I do know: He speaks. Even when you're not tuned in. Even when you're not listening. Even when you're not asking. Even when you're not praying. Even when you're not crying out for help. Even when you're zooming along, cranking the tunes, with your whole life in front of you.

And when he speaks, you should do what he says:

"Stay focused."

"Stay true."

And "Put your seatbelt on!"

Perry here. In 1999, I went to visit Jason, my wife's nephew, and Alan, my wife's brother, in Sao Paulo, Brazil. It was my first serious international trip, and lemme tell ya, Sao Paulo was an eye-opener. Twice the population of Chicago in one-third the space.

One day Alan's friend Paulo Mota took us on a day-long tour of the *favelas*—the slums. My wife, Laura, snapped a picture of this homeless kid, maybe 9 years old, sleeping in a doorway with his dog.

I remember coming home from that trip and saying to myself, "Compared to Sao Paulo, here in Chicago, we've got no pollution, no corruption, no poverty, and no problems of any significance!" I spent the next several weeks processing the whole experience. It transformed my whole perspective.

The homeless Sao Paulo kid sleeping in a doorway with his dog.

We met a 4-year-old girl with severe disabilities who was alive simply because a man from the U.S. offered to pay her medical bills. I don't know whether it was a huge expense for him, but he wouldn't have known about it if he hadn't gone to Brazil.

Laura and I vowed to make regular trips from our cushy Starbucks world to the developing world, so as not to grow numb to the problems of the world. Since then, I've visited many such places and adopted a couple of kids from China.

I believe an important ingredient of hearing memos clearly is caring for those who are less fortunate. Some people get awfully theological and formulaic about "who's in the God club," but most of the teachings by a particular Jewish carpenter about how we'll be judged have to do with how we treat the poor. He said (rather audaciously): how you treat them is how you treat me.

That's why I believe those who care for the poor are also in the best position to hear from the Head Office.

Chapter 13

HEMORRHAGES AND CHRONIC STRESS AT AGE 28

From Jordan Gerding, a business consultant in Eugene, Oregon.

At Oregon State University, I studied construction engineering management because that's what my dad had done. I earned the same degree he'd earned 20 years earlier.

Before college, I had worked in the family business most of my life: a janitor on the weekends, a carpenter through the summers, eventually a project intern and then a project engineer.

But coming out of college, I was torn between going into ministry or staying in the construction business. While I was trying to sort this out, God spoke very clearly through a couple people, "Hey, you know, we really think you're supposed to stay in this business with your dad. Move forward in it and see what God's going to do." So, I stuck with Dad.

In my first year out of college, I attended an Every Nation Church Conference, which is held once every three years. They pull people from all around the globe to this big event. I mean, they even smuggle people out of hostile places like Iran, Pakistan and China and then smuggle them back in—just so they can attend this conference!

So, there I was worshiping with people from 50 countries, and it was powerful. I think it creates an extra "thin space" when you've got so many different people from so many different perspectives all coming together for the same purpose. It's like Heaven and Earth are barely separated.

So, we were worshipping, and I was journaling, and God whispered to me, "Whatever your managers bring up at work for you to do, step up and take it because you're going to be able to do it."

Well, when I returned from the event, the company was having issues with estimates. I'll spare you the boring details, but if you get the estimate wrong in the construction business, it can cost you bucketloads of money. Like millions of dollars. And our estimation process was broken and costing us big time.

So, they asked me to fix it. Standardize it.

I was fresh out of college, taking over a project that could save the company tens or hundreds of millions if I got it right. Or it could cost us millions of dollars if I got it wrong. But, like the Voice told me, I stepped up and took it. Over the next year and a half, I whipped our estimation process into shape, implementing procedures and templates to make it hum.

Once I got those in place, I moved back into the project management arm of the company and oversaw about $25 million worth of work in the next three years. Throughout this time of working hard, grinding my gears, I started wondering again, "Is this really what I want to be doing?"

The work was very stressful, and it got so bad that my body was actually giving out. I was exhausted all the time. At 28 years old, I had a colonoscopy that showed hemorrhages in my large intestine.

In January 2018, the Head Office prodded me to figure out how to use my prophetic gift, my "memos ability" in business. I had not seen it used in business before, only in churches. Every time I thought about it, I remembered the story from Acts in the Bible where the sorcerer saw the apostles using their Holy Spirit abilities and tried to buy them! He was not rewarded for his effort.

A month later, Perry did a promotion in his forum, a Google Group where members of Perry's tribe ask and answer business questions, for Valentine's Day. We were all encouraged to swap services with someone else or just give something away for free. I offered two things. First, I offered some free construction consulting. Nobody took me up on that.

Second, I offered memos. And seven people responded.

One of them, Sean, did not identify as a Christian. Maybe you'd call him a Universalist or something, but he kept hiring me to do more memos, month after month.

And he kept encouraging me: "Jordan, you need to get this out there. This is exactly what the world needs, and no one else is offering it. You need to figure out how to do this all the time."

I agreed and appreciated the encouragement, but I didn't know how!

In August of 2018, I met Melvin Pillay, and discovered someone in the world was integrating business with the prophetic successfully! Awesome! It can be done! So, I started working with Melvin. I did a "whiteboard session" with him; a half-day intensive. And after it was over I thought, "I think I could do this too."

When I got home, I called Sean and asked, "Hey, could I drive down there and do a half-day memos session with you for free? I just want to see if this works."

This was while I was still completely stressed out at my construction gig. Sometimes I could barely make it through the week. I couldn't bear to do anything outside of work. For three weeks, I didn't even buy groceries because I was too exhausted to go to the store.

But I drove three hours to see Sean and had the time of my life holding this half-day session. Not only did it go better than either of us expected, but I also felt a surge of energy, like I'd gotten B-12 injected into my veins!

Anyway, as I was packing up my stuff at the end of the day, Sean said, "Hey, I need to go grab something real quick."

He stepped out of the room and then came back with a check for $600, saying, "This is going to impact the rest of my life; it's worth way more than this check!"

I was thinking, "OK, so not only am I good at this, I enjoy it, and it gives me energy—but I also get paid to do it? This has never happened before."

Immediately, I started thinking about transitioning away from the family business. And I heard the Head Office say, "Let's look at dropping down to 30 hours a week."

So, I went and talked to my dad, the CEO, and said, "I'd like to drop to 30 hours a week."

He said, "I've never let someone moonlight before, so you'll have to talk to the executive team. Realistically, they will probably tell you to either stay on full time, be completely focused on Gerding Builders, or go pack up and do your own thing."

That response surprised me because God had said 30 hours per week—not all or nothing.

Between asking my dad and meeting with the team, I dreamed I was deep-sea fishing down in the Gulf of Mexico. Chris, my best friend and church-startup partner, was with me. Suddenly the water was boiling, and there was something huge underneath the boat. And then my fishing line snapped. Chris looked at me and said, "Why didn't you jump in after that?" I looked at him like, "Are you crazy? I knew it was something good and big, but did you see how it was churning the water? It was massive—and unsafe."

I woke up with new clarity: You need to jump in after it. You need to go after your dream.

Then I met with the two main executives, Brian and Dale. They wanted me to finish the last project that I was working on, but, other than that, I was free. This would bring me below the 30 hours per week I was hoping for, and they wouldn't reduce my salary or my benefits or my shares in the company. They allowed me to take as much time off as I needed, as long I got my project work done. It was a huge blessing!

By the end of 2019, I was ready to go full time in my new career.

Shortly after that dream, Melvin invited me to be part of a certification process he was developing. He wanted me to eventually lead it, to be a successor to him! So, he kept giving me more responsibilities. I worked on an event in Panama with a large Christian organization, involving government officials, the head of the police force and influential business executives. He handed off another event in Ohio, where another CEO asked me to shadow him while he did business reviews of his various departments and locations.

Then, some very strange things happened. First, COVID-19 hit and washed all those events away. Poof. Gone.

But over the course of 2020, other, unrelated business flowed my way. I am cash flow positive.

I'm a very relationally driven person, and I feel mentors, like Melvin, are showing up to teach me and open doors for me. He is establishing me in a role where I can help people and authentically be myself.

And be healthy! I no longer feel like I'm in the burning pitch tar pit of hell!

The way the Voice speaks to me is very natural. If I'm writing, I just write, and more stuff comes. If I'm talking to someone, I just talk and more words come.

On a lighter note, one of the ways I developed my "ear" was by playing online poker. I'd listen and hear whether I should fold or hold. A couple of times, the Voice even told me the exact cards my opponent was holding.

Is that cheating?

Here's another one of my "training exercises." I ask, "God, is this a contacts day or is this an eyeglasses day?" Later, I would know it was a good day to wear contacts because it rained when the forecast was clear!

I recall someone who told me, "God's ready and willing to talk. Don't wait for a crisis to learn how to tune your radio. Stress makes it harder to hear the signal in all the noise." But if you're learning to listen better every day, even with little yes or no questions, you'll hear him even when the thunder is crashing.

And if you have a problem with the idea of God, a specific type of God, I would say, let that idea go. Engage with the Higher Power at whatever level you can engage. If you're comfortable thinking it's an "impersonal force" that's connecting us all, then start there.

I believe God is the true source of love. I believe he wants to set things right. I believe he wants to fill you with life and love and help you bring more of it to others.

If that sounds like good news to you, then start anywhere.

Chapter 14

"HEAVEN IS A PLACE"

From Jo Shaer who runs a digital marketing agency and lives in Essex, England.

I didn't grow up believing in anything spiritual. Nothing. I was a 100% rational, logical, work-hard-all-the-time kinda gal.

In fact, when Perry's "God emails" started coming, I opted out! Nope. Pass. Stick to business, sir.

However, eventually my company joined Perry's Roundtable Europe. Our business was small compared to the other companies in that group, and we didn't know if we really fit in. We were just a struggling pay-per-click digital marketing agency trying to make it work.

Anyway, my partner Jon dove into Perry's 30-Day Reboot program, which really emphasized starting your day with what he calls "Renaissance time": journaling, meditation, reading ancient texts, prayer, etc. And so Jon was keen to get on the Memos from the Head Office calls too.

I was reluctant. To me it sounded like going to a psychic to get your fortune told. Humbug! But since Jon was so enthusiastic, I finally agreed.

Just a note. The Memos from the Head Office calls are webinar calls. You jump on the call, and the memos staff sees only your name. They don't know you. You don't ask them questions. You don't tell them about your business, your life or anything. They just see your name and give you a memo.

Memo: August 2018 (from Gary)

"This is a strange message, but I'm just going to repeat it: "Hey Jo, you need a well-balanced diet—make sure she understands there are other channels of influence. Get outside and strike a balance. This will be a game changer."

As I mentioned, I've always been a nose to the grindstone gal—just keep working and working. But Jon was learning that there are more channels to listen to, and he had been trying to get me to see that too.

We did take this memo seriously, and the message has been one of the most important things we've incorporated into our lives. It has given us permission to go to fun places and do fun things because we get even *more* and *better* work done when we're *not* in the office.

On that first memos call, Julie added: "Head Office is teeing things up for you, as an opportunity. But you need to decide if you're up for the challenge of this. Why not you, and why not now?"

As I mentioned, Jon and I were both pretty insecure about joining Roundtable. "Do we really belong here? Are we big enough?" Julie's memo was like "Wow, how do these people I've never met know all my insecurities? This is kind of alarming."

But we took it as a nod from the universe. "I see you. You can do it. Why *not* you?"

At the September Roundtable meeting in Milan, Italy, Perry told us we should transform our agency from a generic one-size-fits-all agency into one that specializes *only* in fire and security companies.

This made me tremble. Our old way seemed comfortable. Why not just keep working harder in our comfort zone? Limiting our offer to just one industry seemed risky.

But we did as we were told. We "fired" our other clients and changed our website to reflect the new direction. And things started happening—but slowly. We bit our nails to the nub waiting.

Memo: November 2018 (from Julie)

"You're making a mark, and people are noticing."

OK, that boosted my confidence. I gave my nails a break for a while.

Then, in January of 2019, Perry asked us to do a webinar with him to help promote the next year of Roundtable Europe.

Jon and I thought, "Well, we haven't really achieved that much, have we?"

But Perry said: "Let's take a look. When you started Roundtable, you were working like dogs. Even on the weekends. Now you have time to do yoga, go to the beach. You're making the same amount of money now, but you have fewer customers. Fewer hassles. Doesn't that sound like achievement to you?"

Um, yes. Yes, it does.

Memo: January 2019 (from Julie)

"It's all about being different from your competitors."

Remember, these memos folks don't know our business. We're not giving them a synopsis of what we're working on.

We just jump on a call, they see our name and they start giving a memo! Also, the memos people are not marketers either.

So, this memo was another confirmation that the universe is affirming Perry's direction to us to specialize!

In April 2019, at the next Roundtable meeting, Perry said he wanted us to do more than just get leads for fire and security companies. He wanted us to start booking the appointments with the leads for them. And to start offering a money-back guarantee.

Gulp.

I was still not quite convinced we had done the right thing with the specialization strategy, and now he wanted us to dive even deeper with it?! We were not getting many more customers at the time, and there was loads of stuff happening with my family. It was a very stressful time. And Perry was making it more stressful!

Memo: May 2019 (from Julie)

"You know, it's a good thing you don't have people beating down the door because you try to make your work so good that it would be hard to maintain the quality if you had more. But the Head Office is right with you on this, and the inquiries will start when you're ready. You just have to ask for them."

Hmmm. I'm worried about not having enough customers, and the universe is saying, "It's a good thing you don't have more customers because you need this time to get everything right."

It sounds very specific to me. Not mumbo-jumbo stuff that I've got to kind of twist and make it fit to our situation. It is exactly what I was thinking about and worrying about!

Memo: June 2019 (from Gary)

"You need to embrace the message from an old friend. I'm not sure if it's a person, an idea or a thing from the past, but it will tap you on the shoulder; you will recognize it."

Hmmmm. Well, a few days later I started seeing ads on Facebook about a pay-per-lead training we had purchased back in 2018. I won't go into details, but this training fit almost exactly with what Perry was telling us about setting the appointments for our clients and taking over more of their marketing. We needed this training to get our "machine" working right.

I thought, "OK, Gary, let's embrace this old friend." And so, we started that training. It helped us put the machinery in place that we would need to set appointments and make our guarantees.

But by August 2019, the shit was really hitting the fan, and I was getting scared. We were building this machine, but nothing was flowing through it yet. No money was coming in, and I still had to pay all these people, so it was going to come out of my wages or my savings!

I was still fretting over all this when Jon and I sat down to watch *The Handmaid's Tale* on television. That particular episode started very strangely, with Belinda Carlisle singing "Heaven is a Place on Earth."

No music underneath, just her eerie solo voice.

And I can't explain the sensation, but I felt like I heard, "This is a message. Pay attention!" It felt like being smacked in the face.

And both Jon and I felt it.

The show played the whole song at the beginning and then again over the end credits. For days afterward, I couldn't forget the song, and how the lyrics encouraged me to not be afraid anymore.

Then it got really weird.

Memo: August 2019 (from Gary)

"Head Office says there's a song in your head, and they're speaking directly to you through this song."

What?

I had absolutely no doubt what the song was! So, OK, I realized that we were just beginning to understand, and that we were not supposed to be afraid anymore.

Two hours later a huge inquiry came in from the website. We *never* got inquiries through the website. And this was a national fire and safety firm wanting pay-per-lead, which is not even mentioned on the website! They wanted the exact services that Perry had told us to offer.

And we had a system, a machine, in place to actually execute that for them.

You couldn't make this up!

Things went well for a couple of months, but by December we were still struggling to make it work.

Memo: December 2019 (from Gary)

"This memo is all about how you are going to flourish, thrive and prosper in 2020. And many people are going to benefit because of you. You're going to be providing these leads for them."

And from Julie, "Yep, it's about provision, but it's also about permission; you've got to set yourself free and do it your way."

We thought she meant to do it our way, not the way the clients wanted it done.

One client wanted to cash in his money-back guarantee;

he wanted leads from a 17-mile area around his office. Just too small to scale reliably. And another difficult client was also talking about drop-dead dates to see success.

Two potential refunds.

I wasn't sure whether we could renew for another year of Roundtable Europe. In fact, one evening, I finally made up my mind that we would *not* renew. Final answer.

Or so I thought.

Then I picked up Perry's January *New Renaissance* newsletter to cheer myself up.

Halfway through, I discovered a big section all about us, and how we were moving toward dominating fire and security leads. It was all laid out in black and white!

You should have heard me squeal! It had been a dream of ours to get mentioned in the newsletter, and there we were!

One piece of advice in that newsletter stuck out to me: "Build your bionic sausage machine. Just keep yourself alive however you need to, and get the entire process elegant, beautiful and uber efficient."

Exactly what we'd been doing. Our machine was built— but not many sausages yet.

And then a few days later, on a Sunday night, we got another website inquiry.

Again, remember, this doesn't happen often. This lead is a guy in the U.S. who saw us in the newsletter. He's got 500 fire and security companies he wants help with. We would have never gotten that lead without the mention in the newsletter, which, remember, I read immediately after deciding *not* to rejoin Roundtable!

The universe is talking, Jo!

We then completely ripped our website to shreds. We took out anything that wasn't related to fire and security. Removed 1,200 blog posts about generic digital marketing!

The sad, small website left behind now screamed, "Pay-per-lead for Fire and Security!" We made it very easy and obvious for them to speak to us.

And in less than a week, we started getting inquiries from fire and security companies coming in through the contact form.

Suddenly, our online sales funnel was cranking out leads for fire and security. A big national company signed up for a big order. Then another.

Yes, it did look like we would flourish, thrive and prosper in 2020.

So, did we?

The year began very well with three new pay-per-lead customers. And then, well, we all know what happened in early 2020. The pandemic hit, and the bottom dropped out of our pay-per-lead niche.

It was a real rollercoaster financially and emotionally. We had to pay out refunds and had no other money coming in.

But here's the thing. If there had been no pandemic, we would have carried on trying to do pay-per-lead for people who demand the lowest price then bitch about the quality of the lead if it doesn't immediately turn into a sale.

It's a hard, pressurized slog that is not much fun and takes up huge amounts of our time.

The pandemic forced us to go after better clients and gave us the time to serve better clients!

And it's these clients who are showing us that there is a whole different world out there.

They think big and want to try new ways of doing things! It's not just about paid ads flogging an offer that is no different from everyone else's in the niche. It's not about a fatal race to the bottom for the lowest price.

Our new clients want us to help them be different from

their competitors. These entrepreneurs are brave, agile and innovative. They want to use our expertise and experience as partners in their success. To develop creative, courageous ideas to help them create the optimal customer experience.

When we do that type of creative work, we really are thriving.

And in the autumn of 2020 another big client like that signed up.

So, did we flourish financially in 2020? No. But who did? We feel we "survived" 2020 far better than most. And we are thriving—creatively, mentally and emotionally!

Is all this God? The universe? My own intuition? I have no idea, and I don't really care.

All I know is that when I make the time and the space to listen, I hear. And when I was nose to the grindstone, I never heard a thing.

You must get yourself away from your desk. You must go somewhere where you can hear. Wherever that is for you: the beach, the mountains, the shower, yoga, a walk around the block. That's where these ideas flow. Listen!

Put yourself into a space where the Universe, God, whatever you want to call it, is telling you what you need to be doing.

Your to-do list can wait. In fact, the Universe knows what your to-do list *should* be. And if you're not listening, you won't be doing the right things!

Don't worry whether to call this process religion, the Universe, intuition.

When you get an invitation to hear a memo, just accept it!

Chapter 15

NO LABOR PAINS!

From Shae Bynes an author and speaker who runs a consulting business in Lauderhill, Florida.

In 2012, about a month and a half before I started my business, I went to a women's conference in Orlando. On the last day of the conference, the pastor spoke about how God gives us eyes to see things from his perspective and ears to hear his voice.

I thought, "Hmmm, if I'm going to do this entrepreneur thing, that would probably be a really great thing to have! I think I'm going to need that!"

The pastor prayed and asked God to show or speak something to us: just a general picture or word. Then, she had all the women who saw or heard something stand up. I didn't.

So, all these ladies were standing up, and I was feeling irritated and disappointed because I really wanted to "get" something.

Then, as the pastor was making her closing remarks, I just *dropped* to the floor. I could not move a muscle. It felt like a big fat angel was sitting on my back. And I had a vision for the first time in my life.

It was like watching a movie. I saw myself as a child on a playground, playing the trust-fall game. You know, the one where your friends stand behind you, and you just fall back and trust they'll catch you? In my vision, I started to fall, but then I stuck out my arm to brace myself as if I didn't trust the people behind me to catch me.

I heard a voice say, "That's what you do to me!"

I knew this was God talking to me.

He said, "Do you want to know why you do that?"

Yes.

"Because you have absolutely no idea how much I love you."

The next morning, my girlfriend asked me, "So what happened last night?" And as I was telling her, the presence of God showed up. Suddenly I could sense this weight in the room, and I just knew the presence of God was there. I started crying, and my friend did too.

As I was weeping on the floor, I got the second vision: I saw two hands opening and shutting, opening and shutting. I heard a voice say: "This is man—sometimes his hands are open to you, sometimes they're shut. Sometimes they're open. Sometimes they're shut. And you think this is me."

Then I saw a second set of hands—this set was wide open. The voice said, "But this is me. I am your father; I love you. Anything you want, anything you need. I have it. I love you."

After that conference, I kept having similar crazy encounters, one after the other, for two weeks. I was never the same after that. God was so real to me. He didn't feel distant; he had never felt closer.

Laboring in Grace

That was the memo that changed everything in my life. But there were also memos that changed everything in my business. My business is about shifting mindsets and inspiring, teaching and mentoring entrepreneurs who desire to be led by God in their businesses and have kingdom influence in the marketplace.

Around 2014, about a year and a half after I had begun my business, God started talking to me about working not by hustle and grind but by his grace. About a year after that, I felt I was supposed to write a book to help other people shift to work by the power of God's grace.

As I was writing my book, I got pregnant. The Lord said to me, "Don't release the book until the baby is delivered." I got the impression there was something specific and important about my pregnancy that was related to the success of the book.

And the childbirth was nothing short of supernatural— no medication, no pain.

At the point of labor where I was supposed to be going through the most excruciating, teeth-grinding pain, I felt nothing. God told me he wanted to demonstrate what it looks like to "labor in his rest and in his grace," and how this will astound the people around me. So, I put all those experiences in my book.

That was my 10th book, and the Lord told me, through a memo from somebody else, that this would be my breakout book. About a month and a half after I released it, I got a message on Facebook, "Hi, Shae, Have you ever considered doing a Bible reading plan for your book in the YouVersion Bible app?"

I said, no, I had never considered that with this book. I had thought about it a couple of years earlier with other books, but YouVersion was not accepting content partners at the time.

My Facebook correspondent replied, "Well, I believe that you should do it." And then she gave me very specific instructions: "I know the person who's in charge of content partnerships. I'm going to introduce you and recommend you to her. Here's what they're looking for." She didn't tell me at the time that the Lord had told her exactly what to tell me because she didn't want to sound weird.

But her very specific instructions cut through a lot of the hunting and searching and the trial and error I would have needed to do for myself. I went to the app and saw there were several Bible reading plans in the category of "Work." These plans were multiday devotionals where you can give a link to a free e-course at the end.

So, I wrote a reading plan and an e-course, and I got them on the app.

Eventually, I had seven reading plans on YouVersion. So far, I've had almost a half million people follow the plans, and around 38,000 have hopped on my email list.

All that happened in a matter of a few months—with zero marketing budget.

The YouVersion Boost

Then YouVersion put my plan in a "prime spot," moving it to the top of the list for the "Work" category. And it sat in that top space for more than a year. I couldn't have put it there. There's no SEO strategy to try to game, no system to try to manipulate. The app administrators chose to put it there. And so out of all the plans, it produces about 90% of my leads.

Before all this started with YouVersion, I was paying anywhere between $200 to $300 a month on Facebook ads for lead generation. Less than two months later, my company was getting 10 times the number of leads with zero dollars spent on marketing.

And then YouVersion decided to feature one of my plans in a broadcast to their email list. I'm not sure how big the email list was, but millions of people use the app. I couldn't have asked for this placement; I couldn't have paid for it. Someone just picked me!

In that next quarter, everything increased dramatically. Our leads were increasing by eight to 10 times a month. Our mentoring program enrollment more than doubled. Our revenue more than doubled, and the next year it doubled again.

All of a sudden, I was being asked to speak at meetings and conferences, which I had not been doing before. I didn't even have a speaking page or any YouTube videos to promote such a service.

Everything started from the simple message from God: "Do not release this book yet. Wait for me."

When I listened, I was involved in a miracle baby delivery. Then, someone else who was tuned into the Head Office gave me a memo. And, again, when I listened, I was involved in *another* miracle delivery!

These last five, six, seven years have been the best years ever as a result of just listening, taking simple steps and watching his favor flow. It's been amazing.

The full title of my breakthrough book is *Grace Over Grind: How Grace Will Take Your Business Where Grinding Can't*. God said to me, "When you release this book, you're gonna be the poster child for the message in this book." And that has been the absolute truth.

I think that book sold more in the first year than all nine of my other books had sold in five years!

I get memos a lot of ways: when I'm talking to people, when I'm reading the Bible, when I'm doing quiet time, when

I'm journaling. Sometimes I'll write out a question and just listen for the answer. Sometimes memos come to me as I'm driving down the road, taking a walk or taking a shower.

There's nothing "woo-woo" or "coo-coo" about it. It's listening. Anybody can do that.

Perry here again. Some people find that hearing the Voice is as easy as breathing.

Others do not.

For several years I found it quite difficult. I'll never forget the very first time I was put in a position to get a memo. A guy grabbed me and someone else out of a crowd, sat the two of us in front of each other and said, "Go."

It was one of the most uncomfortable things I had ever done. It felt so utterly counter to everything I had ever been taught, to stare at a complete stranger and make some pronouncement "out of thin air."

I went along with it, and it seemed like I might have gotten some of it right, which eased my anxiety. But I wasn't too sure, and it was neither easy nor natural. Later I had more chances to practice. In Chapter 1, I told the story of going to a conference in Ontario where we spent a couple of days practicing. I did get a little better there.

But I still found that when I tried to listen just for myself, to connect with the Head Office simply for my own sake, I rarely got much of anything. But every now and then, some clear message would break through. Usually, it would just be a sentence or two. Every few months I might get an entire paragraph.

At one conference, the organizer described a very useful exercise, which is great for beginners, and will almost always work to some degree. He told us:

> Pick any story from any Scripture you like. It could be a famous story like David and Goliath or the most obscure story you can find. Whether it's a chapter or just a few paragraphs, read it. Then get out your notebook and ask this question:
>
> What would you like me to know about _____?

The name you insert in the blank is either the character you just read about, or else it's you. What would you like me to know about [King David]? What would you like me to know about [me]?

Then GO. Start writing. Write whatever comes. Do not edit. Do not hesitate. Do not compose. Do not question. Do not try to figure anything out. Just stream whatever comes next.

At that time, I felt I was in a personal dungeon of weighty stuff I simply did not know how to overcome. For a couple of years, I had tried to wriggle free, but I couldn't go over, under, through or around. Couldn't go forward; couldn't back up. The passage I opened to was about Samson, the strong guy who became weak when Delilah nagged him until he let her cut his hair, as described here in the book of Judges:

> She made him go to sleep on her lap and then called a man in to shave off the seven braids of his hair. She made him vulnerable, and his strength left him. She said, "The Philistines are here, Samson!" He woke up and thought, "I will do as I did before and shake myself free." But he did not realize that the Lord had left him. The Philistines captured him and gouged out his eyes. They brought him down to Gaza and bound him in bronze chains. He became a grinder in the prison.[7]

I read that and wrote, "Tell me about Samson." Then I started writing, and this is what flowed effortlessly from my pen:

> Delilah is seducing him, her silver tongue. Jesus says to me, I watched over Samson, and I knew where all this was headed. I knew they would tear his eyes out (I would feel it too). I knew how it would all play out. I knew the legacy he would leave, crushing the temple of Dagon and the mark upon his soul. And his cry for God in the Dungeon, his lost destiny and the hopes of his parents, his consecration and his vows. I knew it all.

---

7 Judg. 58:5-8 NET

I knew destinies would be fulfilled through his example. As I looked through the ages, I saw that he would strengthen men and women. I gave him the jawbone of the ass, and I have given it also to you to steal, kill & destroy the works of evil. I have disciplined you in the dungeon and given you sight for the blind that those who worship vain things will suddenly see my glory.

I stared at my paper. "Did I really just write that?" It had come so easily. It was so encouraging. *Dude, I know you feel like you're in a dungeon right now. Stick with me. There's a bigger plan in play. We'll get through this.*

You can try that exercise too. At any time.

Or you might try variations of the same exercise. When COVID body-slammed the world in 2020, I invited my clients to start their day by asking this question: "OK. You've got my attention now. What do you want me to know?"

And even if you just get one solitary word—a word like "courage" or "comfort" or "lament" or "persist"—take that word and meditate on it.

You can hold on.

If you would like to get your own Memo from the Head Office from my team, register at www.perrymarshall.com/morememos

Chapter 16

THE CAFFEINE-FREE DOWNLOAD

From Olivier Duong, a Haitian-French-Vietnamese photographer and marketer who lives in Margate, Florida.

My mother was diagnosed with cancer when I was 10. She had part of her lung and part of her brain removed. One day, she came home with a shaved head and a big scar. I didn't recognize her.

For several months before she passed, I lived with a nagging feeling in my chest. I knew, "One day I will pass by her room, and she won't be breathing."

Every time I passed by, I checked. Waiting for the day. Of course, she eventually died. I believe those "waiting days" were where my struggles with anxiety were born.

Fast forward many years. Now I'm in business, and my anxiety has morphed into a sinking feeling about my email inbox. Every time an email popped up, my mind would leap to, "Oh no! What's wrong? What's going to happen? What will I find in this email?"

To avoid being paralyzed by fear, I turned off email notifications and determined to check emails only three times a week. And yet the dread remained. Every single time it was time to check, and even the moments in between, I'd get a cold shiver down my back.

I always wondered, "What terrible incident is waiting for me in my inbox today?"

I delegated my emails to an assistant, but that only seemed to increase my anxiety further! Now I worried, "Can he actually handle the emails? What's he going to screw up? Will the cure be worse than the disease?"

For a control freak, which is what I was, releasing control to someone else does not usually help.

So, I wrenched back control of my email. I would finish my workweek on Friday. Then on Saturdays, I would stay away from my main work and do pet projects. Sundays I would rest.

But then on Sunday around 5 or 6 p.m., the sharp pains would start, the panic attacks. "There's an email waiting for you that's going to destroy your whole business!" One moment I would be happy, playing with my family, and in the next second, my fragile anxiety bubble would burst, and I'd be in full panic mode.

Crippling.

One day, I was in a hotel room in Thailand on vacation, and my son got sick. Puking every 30 minutes sick. Our vacation was ruined, and my panic attacks about email were jacked up to 11.

I was losing it.

I just broke down: "I can't live like this! I really, really cannot live like this. Why continue in business if I always feel so out of control?"

It didn't make any sense. I'm a very rational person. Rationally, I knew if there were 100 emails, maybe one person would be upset, but I could deal with that. Yes, occasionally someone would say something mean and ask for a refund. But for every client like that, I had 20 to 30 people raving about my awesome products.

Why couldn't I focus on the glowing reviews instead of the one complainer? But no amount of rational thought can calm irrational fears.

So, I broke down, but, as I was breaking down, I heard God say, "Do not fear."

I heard him say those words over and over.

So, I thought: "OK, 'do not fear' means 'do something else' about it. I need to *do* something about this. And I'm going to do it today."

And so, I prayed.

Do you know what I "heard?"

It sounds silly, but my memo very clearly was:

"Cut coffee."

The memo did not come from an audible voice. But the words were clear, as though written in front of me in bold letters on a white piece of paper.

"Well, I prayed and asked for direction, and I got a direction. It's a *weird* direction, but whatever."

So, I did it.

Here's where the story gets good.

After three days of cutting coffee, I faced my Sunday email ritual, the one I normally dreaded. After I finished with the email, I went back to watch cartoons with the kids.

And while I was watching cartoons, I got a "divine hot seat": very specific instructions about what to do next.

I couldn't get back to my computer fast enough. I knew exactly what I needed to do. In my business, I sell online photography courses, and suddenly I saw the steps I needed to take—one by one and in specific order—to fix everything in my sales funnel:

"#1: Put your front-end product here. #2: Sell it at this price. #3: Test it at this price afterward. #4: This is what your upsell should be. #5: Then put this product here."

All the things that I needed to do—a full game plan—had come to me in a split second. I made all those changes as fast as I could and sent an email to my list with the new "funnel."

Five sales arrived in the first 10 minutes.

"Wow, I can already tell this is going to work."

It was like there had been a kink in the water hose that I could not see. As soon as it got straightened out, water started flowing again.

I had been seeking an answer about my anxiety over my email, but I got way more.

I had often prayed, "God, please help the business," in a generic sense. But for some reason, it never clicked in my brain that I should pray about specific things in the business. I didn't know I should pray about conversions, upsells, products, pricing—stuff like that.

I have retained a lucidity about my business that I didn't have before. I am more able to see the 10,000-foot overview. A lot of times, you put your nose to the grindstone, and you're not really aware of what you're doing. You're working in your business, not on your business. But now, I can see what's not working, and I can see what I need to fix at every turn.

Why did the Head Office have me cut coffee? I don't know. I had never had any problems with coffee, and I'd been drinking it since I was a kid. I had never thought I was drinking "too much" or that it might be tied to my anxiety.

I think the coffee directive was less about the caffeine and more about me asking for guidance, getting the impression of an idea in my head and being obedient to it.

I am Haitian, so our normal drink is espresso. Strong coffee. Surprisingly, I did not have terrible withdrawals from going completely off coffee, cold turkey. Just a general headache that was manageable and didn't last.

Then, 10 days later, I felt like the Head Office was saying, "OK, that's enough, you can go back to coffee."

In the 10 days I cut coffee, the panic attacks vanished. And they never returned.

Weird, I know. And I don't know exactly what to think about it all. But here's what I think I do know. First, the Higher Power is interested in what you're doing, so ask about it.

Second, when you ask, be specific, don't just ask about general things. Ask, "How can I fix the conversions on my front-end product?" Not, "Please bless me."

He wants to get his hands dirty in the details of your life.

Chapter 17

SHE ROARS

From Carla Pratico, a marketing consultant and business adviser who lives in New York City.

I won a bunch of awards in high school and was named Woman of the Year at Virginia Tech when I graduated in 2009. But I never intended to be an entrepreneur. I expected the accolades on my résumé to help me climb the corporate ladder.

I moved to New York to apprentice with a leadership consultant who was working with Burberry, Ferragamo and American Airlines. I was on my way up the ladder, I thought.

Then I started having God encounters.

During one of these encounters, he showed me a business I was supposed to start—with him. "I'm your partner. I'm your co-founder, co-CEO." It was going to be a prophetically led, Spirit-driven business.

So, I quit my corporate gig and fired it up—with him.

My workday looked like this: From nine to noon was "Renaissance time"—meditating on Scripture, prayer, worship and learning business from Scripture. I studied Scripture for a solid three years, several hours each day, learning how to build a business based on what the Spirit was showing me.

Holy Spirit MBA?

Then in 2012, a client asked me to create a marketing strategy for her. She was a demanding client. High standards and very little grace. I got to work putting together a proposal, but I got stuck when it came time to decide what to charge her. So, I asked my "business partner." And I heard the Head Office say, "I want you to charge $2,500. Not a penny less."

I had never heard the Head Office give me specific instructions like that before—very direct, very specific. So, I followed orders, priced it at $2,500, and fired it off to the client.

She emailed me back. "Let's go ahead and get started for $2,000."

She assumed, me being young and needing the money, that I'd just accept her lowball. And I almost did. I mean, I did need the money. Why quibble over $500 when I could add $2,000 to my bank account?

But my business partner had said, "Not a penny less."

God had always seemed so gentle and kind in his "words" to me over the years. I had gotten used to that soft touch. But this time he was like a stern father. He was daddying me. He was showing me how to stand my ground.

"Remember what I told you? You need to insist on your pricing. You need to stand up for what you sent her. You need to do what I said, right?"

So, I emailed her back, "I know the standard of excellence that you have. And there's really no way for us to scale back the project to get the desired results that you're asking for. Because of that, we really can't go with a lower price point."

I was 23 years old, and I was so nervous. I had no idea what I was doing; I was just sort of following the Voice. I was also acutely aware that my bank account could really use a $2,000 influx. For the next week, I was on the edge of my seat waiting for this woman to email me back.

Finally, she replied, "Carla, you're worth every penny you charge. We'll circle back to you when we're able to afford you."

I thought, "Hmmm. She used the same language God used: 'You're worth every penny you charge.'"

That was a very significant moment for me. At the time, it took courage for me to ask for $2,500. Heck, I probably would have been happy with $500! I had enough experience to know I could deliver, but I certainly didn't know much about negotiation or sales or being confident about charging and making a profit.

And here God comes and says, "Not a penny less." And he was so stern about it. I wasn't used to him putting his foot down. So, it made me put my foot down and stand up straight.

That day he "leveled-up" my business. From that point on, I didn't play in the hundreds anymore. I played in the thousands. I went from charging $2,000 to charging $10,000 and $20,000 for web design. His voice smashed through my fear of charging more—of charging what I'm worth. And I never went back.

And he taught me a very important lesson. When you level up, you can't always take your old clients with you. And that's OK. In fact, you may need to let them go to make room for the bigger clients. Without letting the little ones go, you never get the big ones.

I look back at that one moment and see that thousands of dollars have flowed to me from that one decision. But more than that, it's enabled me to see my value as a woman. And I now train women to build their own businesses with God through my organization: She Roars.

Adderall Aftermath

During my college years and the early years of my business career, I got addicted to Adderall.

I started using it, like too many college kids do, as a "study aid." But if you know anything about Adderall, you know it's a stimulant. It helps you laser focus. It's basically legalized speed. You can become reliant on it to the point where you have zero energy without it.

Soon, I was relying on it just to function, and I was hooked for 10 years. I got up to 80 milligrams a day. Then, in 2013, I was supernaturally delivered from my addiction. That full story is too long to tell here. I want to talk more about what happened afterward.

While I was on the drug, I was functional, if not healthy. I focused on building my client list and paying my two employees. And I was able to tread water.

After my deliverance from the drug addiction, my body needed recovery time—it just did not want to function without its preferred fuel source. I stayed in bed 16 hours a day, sometimes more, not wanting to even get up and eat.

Yes, I had two employees, but my business was not set up to function without the boss. Not being able to work meant not enough money coming in. So, I had to lay off those two employees and brace for the worst.

My parents would have bailed me out financially, but I

felt like I was being instructed not to share what was going on with them, and instead to walk this thing out with him.

Things got really tight financially. Just before I laid off my assistant, I sent her out for groceries. I had made a very specific list based on what was in my bank account. She bought one extra item, a box of Saran Wrap. "Nope! You have to return that now—it's going to overdraft my bank account!" Saran Wrap. Like $1.50, right? Living on the edge.

So, I laid off my employees and stayed in bed. I was totally tanking financially, eating up every morsel of savings. I felt such shame. I felt like my bank account was my identity, so my identity was *zero*. I was nothing.

Now and then, I would land a client who would sustain me for a couple weeks, but I was barely able to squeak out the work. After about 10 months, my body finally started to recover, and I started landing big contracts. I felt like God was guiding me, telling me which "doors to knock on," which people to pitch.

The Shame of Shame

But I was months behind on rent. I went to housing court four times to delay my eviction. The next phase would have been where they order a court martial to come and post the "You gotta be out by Friday, or we're kicking you out" notice on my door.

During this time, I heard God say to me: "You know it's not *my* will that you're in this place. It's *shame* that you got here. I never intended for you to be almost homeless, never intended for you to walk through all this stuff."

Shame, huh? OK.

So, that week I finally decided to tell people what was going on. I sent an email to a core group of friends, and, within two days, two people offered to cover all my back rent. Their generosity broke the curse of shame off of my business identity.

I didn't realize how much shame had been controlling my decision making and my communication with people. Once I shared what was going on, it was like everything broke open for me.

The court martial was coming on a Friday. On Thursday, my friends had given me enough money to pay off my whole back rent. An 11th-hour intervention.

Over the next 12 months, I went from a negative bank account to building a six-figure business—working only 20 hours a week.

I believe a lot of this was connected to healing the shame in my own heart, not confusing my business with my identity, and realizing I'm a leader regardless of what my bank account says.

You probably want to know, "How did you hear God?" When I hear from God, it's an all-day conversation. When I heard those words, I wasn't really journaling or specifically praying for advice.

For me, the famous scripture "Pray without ceasing"[8] is my guiding light. It means the floodgates are always open. There's no specific time or place allocated for him to speak to you. He's everywhere, all the time.

My breakthrough wasn't a lightning bolt moment, other than when the Head Office told me: "You need to share what's going on in your life with those around you; shame has been causing you to make bad decisions and hide."

He told me not to share with my parents because if they had bailed me out it would not have given us—God and me—the space to deal with the real issue: my shame.

I think everybody hears from God. Usually, we call it intuition, where you just "know" something, yet there's

8 1 Thessalonians 5:17

no rational reason for you to know it. If you really sit back and think about intuition, it's the same as the sense we have that there is a creator who is all-knowing and speaks to his creation in order to help us out.

And he will bang the cymbals louder if you need them to be louder. If you're willing to listen, he'll do what he needs to for you to get the memo.

It's worth testing the waters, dipping your toes in and saying: "You know what? If you're real, and you're really good, show me what you're like. Show me who you are and speak to me. I want to hear what you have to say."

Pick up your bonus material, reading list, and all the appendices free at www.perrymarshall.com/morememos.

Chapter 18

HEAD TRASH ABOUT A ROLEX DATEJUST 41

From Melvin Pillay, an author, speaker, sales trainer and business adviser who lives in Fairview, Texas.

I've always believed in the power of prayer. I've always believed God loves me. I've always believed God knows a lot about business.

And I thought I had broken free from the "poverty mentality" or the "poverty spirit" a long time ago.

God had been working on me for about a decade, breaking me away from the guilt of spending money on myself. I could always spend on others, spend money on clients, take people to five-star restaurants and hotels. That was all fine as long as it was money spent on somebody else. But not me.

God had been teaching me for over 10 years that I needed to stop thinking that way. So, I thought I had reached that place where finally, the poverty mentality was broken, and I could invest in myself without feeling guilty.

But in March 2019, I was in Las Vegas, and I felt the Lord was teaching me something brand new. He was teaching me about the power of angels.

Angels had been a topic I shied away from because of all the many nutty things some people say. But God was teaching me a lesson, and I had an impression that angels were there to help me in business and finance.

I was walking in Caesar's Palace with my wife, and I said to God, "Lord, in the areas of angels, I'm really uncomfortable and concerned—I don't want people to think that I'm some sort of loony guy."

Then he directed me to a Scripture in the Book of Hebrews that describes angels as "ministering spirits sent to serve those who will inherit the everlasting inheritance." I said, "OK, God, if this is true, let something tangible happen in my life, which I can then teach to others."

As we walked through the hotel, the Lord very clearly prompted my heart:

"Walk into the Rolex store."

I went inside and greeted the salesman of all salesmen. He located the most gorgeous Rolex watch, put it on my hand, and said to Michele, "Doesn't this watch look so beautiful on him? Doesn't it make him feel like a billionaire?"

Man, this guy could sell it! This guy was incredibly professional too. He was very confident and not at all sleazy or shifty. I knew I was in trouble because that watch was beautiful. It fit me and my personality perfectly.

The price? $15,000!

Michele said, "Go ahead, Melvin. Buy this watch."

And I said under my breath, "Keep your poker face, come on! Don't let on to this guy about how much you want this watch."

I said to the salesman, "Listen, I love it, but we'll come back another time."

I whispered to my wife, "Michele, if the Lord wants me to have this watch, I'm not taking $15,000 from our savings. The Lord will provide the exact amount of money for me to buy this watch."

So, we left.

That evening, I was in one of the high-rise buildings in Vegas, looking down. It was about 2 o'clock in the morning, and I could see guys coming and going in their sports cars, looking for love or passion at strip clubs, night clubs and escort services.

My heart was crying, just breaking for these guys. Because I am not deceived by the surface trappings. I well know that sort of life, while glamorous on the outside, is sad, lonely and soulless on the inside.

I said to the Lord, "My heart is breaking for these people."

Then, all of a sudden, God whispered to my heart, "Melvin, I love you that much. I am your father. I have so much compassion and love for you."

In other words, as I was feeling compassion for those strutting alpha males on the Vegas strip, the Lord was showing compassion for me on a whole different level.

Then he brought the Rolex back to my mind. I felt him say to me, "I want you to have that watch."

I said, "OK, but if you want me to have this watch, release your angels to bring me $15,000 to buy that watch."

Later that day, I got a call from a guy who was referred to me by one of my clients. I'd never met him before. He said to me, "Melvin, a friend of mine told me about these whiteboard sessions you do, and I want to talk to you about it.

"I want to sign up for $15,000 worth."

The money cleared. Exactly $15,000.

But you know what? I still didn't buy the watch!

Michele said, "Melvin, you received the money. Just like you asked. Buy the watch."

But I said, "I can invest that money and watch it grow, so why would I want to buy a watch?"

More Signs

Several months later, we were back in Vegas. Michele has a bank account just for her own shopping, so I checked to see how much was left in that account: about $3,000.

We walked into the Rolex store again because I could not forget about that watch. So, I said to the Lord, "God, if you want me to have this watch, go and command your angels to bring me the $15,000 for this watch."

As God is my witness, and Michele was standing there, I logged out of that account and then logged back in. There was $15,000 in the account!

Michele said, "God has given you this money. Take it! Let's go buy the watch!"

But I *still* couldn't spend the $15,000 on the watch. I just couldn't.

So off we went—again.

About a month later, we were in Dallas. The Lord touched my heart again, "Buy the Rolex watch!"

And then God gave me a *third* $15,000. We had set aside $15,000 for our 10-year anniversary, a big European trip. But due to unforeseen circumstances, we had to cancel at the last minute, so the money was now available.

"It's a sign, Melvin. Buy the Rolex," Michelle said. It turns out that she had been secretly praying for several years that I would have a Rolex by our 10th anniversary."

So, we started hunting for the watch in other places as we traveled: Dallas, Florida, Chicago, Colorado, Utah. We didn't see it anywhere. Michele and I started to call it the "Loch Ness Watch."

That particular watch—a Datejust 41, oyster perpetual in white gold—is extremely rare. We would call the Rolex stores to ask if they had this model, and they would laugh at us. There was a loooong waiting list for that watch. One woman told us a customer had paid for one eight months earlier and was still waiting for it to come in.

Just Because

Finally, our travels took us back to Vegas.

Michele said, "Melvin, it's our 10th anniversary. I am buying this watch for you!"

We landed in Vegas on Saturday and took a walk. There were four or five Rolex outlets in town, and Michele had called all of them. They said, "This watch is impossible to find."

Eventually, we went to the Bellagio and discovered a tiny Rolex store there. And there was the Loch Ness Watch. Sitting right up front in the window!

The woman behind the counter said, "Yes, these are very rare, but two of them came in last night. In fact, I just put this one in the window right before you arrived. Grab it now or it will be gone tomorrow!"

So, we did.

I had asked God for a memo. To release his angels and give me $15,000.

He did it *three times*.

Yet even then, I still wasn't able to swipe the card. I needed Michele to do it for me!

I was praying about this later, and God said to me,

"I want you to understand this. I gave you the watch just because, no condition. I love you because I love you. I want you to have the watch."

My Rolex Datejust 41.

Then the Holy Spirit said to me, "Every time you look at your watch, I want you to remember how valuable you are and how valuable time is."

Remember, even someone who hears memos every day (me!) can be slow to act. None of us gets it right all the time.

But whether you get it right or not, God loves you. Just because.

Participate in a live Memos session and get a free personal listening guide at www.perrymarshall.com/morememos.

Chapter 19

WHY IS IT SO HARD TO BE KIND TO OURSELVES?

PERRY HERE. THE PREVIOUS CHAPTER BY Melvin is strange to me. That's because when someone says "Rolex," I think, "A Rolex is what sleazy televangelists buy after they've fleeced Social Security checks from little old ladies with blue hair."

My inner engineer chimes in and adds, "And I'm not even sure whether Rolexes keep accurate time or not."

Rolex is such a stereotypical status symbol that I found it bizarre to get this piece from Melvin when I started casting about for stories for this book. I have zero interest in wearing a Rolex, but I've got my own version of this story.

I mentioned a guy named Ivan Allum back in Chapter 1. The late Ivan Allum, actually. I met him on several occasions, and in 2010, he gave my wife, Laura, and me a memo.

He said, "Perry and Laura, I've got two words for the two of you: *all inclusive.*"

Ivan explained, "You guys work so hard, and you're responsible for so many things. Heaven is telling me, you need to find one of those places where you stay, and they do *everything* for you. Where you do not have to do anything or think about a single detail. *All inclusive.*"

Oh my, did that ever sound so good.

But it didn't actually happen for eight years!

Now, we did take Ivan seriously. Sort of. I bookmarked that conversation and clearly recall that maybe a year later we took a trip to New Orleans and rented a condo. Fantastic trip. But it was not an all inclusive, and it did not come with servants or staff.

Breakfast was not prepared for us; we went out to restaurants. The afternoon we arrived, we stopped at a grocery store and bought some snacks.

So, vacation? Absolutely.

All inclusive? No.

Why didn't we do it the way Ivan said?

For a whole bunch of bothersome reasons. First, as all parent-entrepreneurs know, clearing your schedule, securing child care and completely exiting everything for even as little as a weekend is a major production. So, it's incredibly easy for months or years to slip by.

I also knew that my very frugal operations manager would frown on such a trip, even if he didn't say anything. We were aggressively trying to grow the business, which required us to constantly reinvest, and I knew he would think, "Why are Perry and Laura taking a four-day, all-inclusive vacation in Cabo San Lucas, when Perry knows we ought to be putting more money into Facebook ads?"

All entrepreneurs have some area of business where more investment would do long-term good. I don't recall any time during that period when we had so much extra money and so few projects (or charities) crying for attention that we would jump up and say, "Let's spend a bunch of money on a luxury vacation!"

In 2010 our life was in a decent spot, and a trip like that would have worked well. But Adoption #1 happened in 2011, along with some other challenges. And there was Adoption #2 in 2015. So, there was a five-year stretch where getting away together was well nigh impossible.

Ivan's instruction kept nagging me, however, and finally in 2018, we worked in a true-blue, all-inclusive trip to Irish Hollow near Galena, Illinois. It was splendid.

Dang. It only took eight years to do something we should have acted on in eight weeks.

LOOKING FOR THE WHY

Please, dear reader, keep in mind that right now I am working hard to articulate why I didn't act on Ivan's memo. Most of the time, we don't really articulate anything. We just live inside our chattering brains and seldom stop to sort ourselves out.

Hard-driving, highly conscientious, type-A leaders often have a very hard time buying perks for ourselves that we cannot rationally justify. And of course, most entrepreneurs go without all luxuries for years just to get businesses off the ground. We're used to it.

So, for many of us, if we're waiting for a convenient time for an all-inclusive vacation to show up, we're going to be waiting a long time.

Which is to say, when you get a memo and know you're supposed to do something, don't assume everything is just going to neatly fall together. Don't expect that rainbows will suddenly appear, your schedule will magically open up and the dinero will drop in your lap.

All those things might happen. But it's just as likely that you will have to fight to take action on the memo.

Laura and I have to discipline ourselves to occasionally do things that restore our sanity, our health, our relationship and our sense of peace and calm.

Many of you reading this book are workaholics who only feel worthy when you are making sacrifices for larger goals and other people. You are uncomfortable doing things for yourselves. And while I find entrepreneurs overall to be very generous people, I think young moms suffer the most from this spirit of sacrifice.

When you have small children, you are sacrificing yourself 24/7/365, many times with zero breaks at all for months!

Laura needs a day or two away every couple of months, either alone or with a friend or two. It's a huge lift to her spirits. And it likely will not happen at all unless the kids and I work together to make it happen.

THE NEED TO RECHARGE

Most breakthroughs in the 21st century are mental breakthroughs: new ways of seeing things, new ways of breaking down a problem. Seldom is any breakthrough purely a result of pressing your shoulder to the wheel even harder. Redoubling your efforts and working more is rarely the answer. Breakthroughs simply do not happen while you're just grinding away.

I've discovered that there are very specific things that I need to do to recharge. This is doubly important because my business requires me to create new things on a regular basis. It is not possible to be brilliant and creative if your inner artist is always gasping for breath.

I've been building stereo equipment since I was 13 years old, and some of the best creative spaces for me occur when I'm designing and building something new. About five years ago, I was journaling one morning when the Head Office said very clearly to me: "Perry, if you're fantasizing about a new design or a better set of speakers, order the parts, get the shipment and start. You do not need to justify, rationalize, or wait until you have achieved some business goal or anything else."

Just get your project started and *go*.

I thought, "That sounds nice—but I've got speakers all over the house. It's not like I need more speakers! What am I going to do with them?"

"Doesn't matter. Give them away to friends. I'll even tell you who to give them to. You just need to design and build them because you are exercising your inner artist. When it's 1:30 in the morning and your project is coming together like a stir-fry, that's when you get your best insights, ideas and epiphanies."

All of which was true. I teach a marketing model called Maze 2.0, which is a method of blending multiple forms of paid social media together, along with a "media map" for visualizing relationships between 50 media channels. The Maze concept came to me at precisely one of those moments I just described—at 1:30 in the morning.

So, I forcibly give myself permission to do this work.

Every project is different. Each pushes me into new regions of my technical and artistic abilities. Very few things get me into flow better than that.

It is not even an expensive hobby. After all, I'm buying wholesale electronic parts, not finished goods in some pricey audio salon. I have a ton of fun doing it and end up with valuable equipment, which I find very interesting and productive uses for. Including gifts.

A Thin Place

I got a very similar memo regarding my regular trips to Ireland. On my third trip there, about seven years ago, I realized, "Every single time you go to Ireland, you have some kind of spiritual epiphany."

Ireland for me is a "thin place," a locale where Heaven and Earth are close together. A place where memos come remarkably easily. Ireland shifts me into flow. Give me hiking boots and a rental car, and the cares of the world are left behind.

That memo was a lot like the stereo equipment memo: "Perry, when you need to go to Ireland, *just go*. You don't need any excuse, reason or rationalization. When you sense you need the head space, buy the plane tickets and go."

Laura knows this too. One time she asked, "Perry, when's your next trip to Ireland?"

"I don't know."

She scowled at me.

By the end of the week, I had purchased the plane tickets.

I do a fairly decent job of taking care of myself, in large part because my wife, who is a very wise woman, goes out of her way to make sure that happens. She's more generous than I am. She knows emotionally and spiritually starved people can't serve other people, can't write impactful books, can't create world-changing companies. Top performers need down time. "All work and no play makes Jack a dull boy."[9]

I manage to get myself to Ireland about three times a year. Sometimes, it's pure vacation. Often, I work it in with other meetings in Europe. Without doubt those trips are among the most valuable and productive things I do. There's nothing like standing on a cliff in front of the mighty surging Atlantic and feeling the wind's furious intensity. Time vanishes, and it's just me and the waves and God.

Melvin's Datejust 41 oyster perpetual in white gold has a very, very specific meaning and history to Melvin. Every time he glances at it, the hands of his watch come with a message. (Including the fact that God gave him $15,000 *three different times* before he let his wife buy it for him.)

Most folks will have a hard time feeling sorry for a guy who can't bring himself to buy a Rolex. Well, nobody's asking you to feel sorry for him. Melvin regularly consults people with eight-, nine- and ten-figure net worths, including heads of state. So, if a guy working in those circles is uncomfortable wearing a Rolex—that actually is a problem.

Head trash is head trash is head trash. At every level.

My latest Dipole speakers, cut out of a slab of live-edge birch I bought at a sawmill in Nebraska, have a very, very specific meaning and history to me. I did a December trip to the Dingle Peninsula where the wind was blowing 40 miles an hour and the ocean was raging at Clogher Beach. I lay back against a cliff, barely out of the wind, and watched the intensity and blowing foam for an hour. Mesmerized by the ferocious power of nature.

---

9 Kubrick, Stanley. 1980. *The Shining*. United States: Warner Bros.

You cannot produce brilliant work if you do not take good care of yourself and feed your artistic and creative engine. But we human beings are inclined to starve and punish ourselves into succeeding. This does not work.

If Melvin's Rolex story rubs you the wrong way, ask yourself if you have a tendency to not take care of yourself.

Do you demur when Heaven offers you an occasional strawberry?

DOES GOD WANT YOU TO BE SUCCESSFUL?

A COMMON OBJECTION I GET TO memos is that they generally tend to be so positive. Hey, isn't the big guy upstairs mad at me? Doesn't he need to get some nasty stuff off his chest before he starts blessing me? Are these people just tickling my ears?

A lot of people suspect that if God appeared and spoke to them in public, he would rip them a new one for all their inadequacies.

Well, how often did Jesus do that when he met someone new?

Jesus did rip a few people to shreds without remorse or apology. But not many. If you're not quite sure which ones and why, I suggest you crack open the book of Luke or John and find out for yourself. It's eye-opening.

Most readers of this book are entrepreneurs. In my opinion, most entrepreneurs (regardless of religious persuasion) exercise more faith every single day than 95% of "people of faith." Faith is stepping off the ledge. Taking risks. Leaping into the void and finding a place to land. Few consider that entrepreneurial faith and religious faith might be more alike than different.

If you're an entrepreneur, and you struggle with the notion of faith, I invite you to consider that choosing to believe there is a Head Office that has good intentions for you is hardly any different from choosing to believe that you'll meet payroll next Friday.

I got the following question from Victor, a young guy struggling to put his business together and to reconcile "greed" with "doing good." He comes from a particular religious persuasion, as you'll see here, but I've never met any particular kind of person from any faith or culture who doesn't somehow struggle to answer these kinds of questions. Even if you don't share Victor's convictions, you will probably still relate.

> **Victor:** If I was to state my life mission in an exact order, I would say that I want to serve God and my fellow man and be financially free. My problem, though, is that I always have this habit or need to immediately justify the financial part, as if it needs to be eliminated from the picture. But I'm trying to save it.
>
> I was raised to always remember that the love of money is the root of all evil, but my question is, "What does that truly mean? What is love of money and where do I draw the line? Am I lying to myself when I want to serve God and man with the help of money?"
>
> **Perry:** When I was in Amway, people liked to say things like, "God wants you to be successful!" "God wants you to drive a Cadillac and live in a mansion!"
>
> Whenever I heard that I would just cringe. I would think, "Dude, how do you know what God wants for me— or anybody else for that matter?"
>
> At the same time, even though hearing these people tell me that God wanted me to be rich was like fingernails on a chalkboard, I would turn right back around and ask myself this question, "OK, Perry, so if you don't believe God wants

you to be successful, then why are you working your ass off to succeed?"

Dear reader, if you're going to be successful in business, you're gonna have to come up with a good answer to that question: "Why are you working so hard?" Until you have an answer that you can fully embrace with all your heart, you will manage to sabotage yourself somehow, some way. And go around in circles and live a tortured existence of lame excuses and indecision.

A lot of people murder their own business success because they are ambivalent about being successful.

If you have in your heart a drive for excellence, a desire to be influential, a desire to go where no one has gone before, a desire to transcend the limitations of being "broke" or not having enough resources; a desire to give more than most people give; a desire to go places most people don't go; a desire to express your individualism, then you *must* figure this out. There is no escaping this question.

A HOST OF ALTERNATIVES

For me, the starting point was asking this question: "What's the alternative?"

There are many alternatives, you know.

1. You can take a vow of poverty.
2. You can be an activist, a monk, a missionary or a Mother Teresa.
3. You can be solidly middle class.
4. You can punch the clock 40 hours a week and take whatever you get.
5. You can set your heart's deepest desire on getting rich.
6. You can simply work to be as excellent as you can be at

what you do with no particular concern about how many rewards you get.

7. You can make a list of life goals and dreams, whatever they may be, and work to create a business that supports those goals and dreams.

Which one is the truly noble path?

I seriously considered all of the above. I know people who have literally followed the first couple of items on this list. They live in places like Mozambique and Kolkata, India, and devote their entire lives to vocations such as running orphanages.

I cannot possibly overstate the respect I have for these people. If it's true that the first shall be last and the last shall be first, then these folks are going to be in the front of the front of the line when it's time to greet Saint Peter at those pearly gates.

I'm dead serious. If your heart is telling you to do something similar, if that's your calling, then do it now and do it without hesitation.

If you do #3 or #4 simply because those paths appear to make the "tough questions" go away, then you're just ducking responsibility. I have no problem with living #3 and #4 if you really and truly have a good reason to do so. But for most people, these alternatives represent mediocrity and wholesale avoidance. Even Jesus promised to spit out the lukewarm people, the ones who were neither hot nor cold.

Alternative #5—getting rich. I'm not a huge fan. I'm sure it's a perfectly good option for some people. But I don't personally believe in pursuing money purely for money's sake. Surely you can find more reasons than that for whatever it is you do. I think pursuing this alternative is often exasperating, and people can easily wear themselves out chasing dollars.

However, if #5 has a powerful appeal for you, run—do not walk— run and buy a copy of *How to Get Rich* by Felix Dennis. The book will inform you of all the pros and cons, and Dennis minces no words. (He even tells you about the time when he had 14 mistresses on the payroll.) He'll also give you some very sound advice.

I've always been intrigued by #6. I didn't really understand it at first; I just knew I liked it. When I was in junior high and high school, I built stereo equipment. It was my first business. But it was more than a business—it was a total fascination and obsession.

I spent endless hours studying the designs of various manufacturers like B&W®, KEF®, Klipsch®, Quad®, Duntech®, Bose®, Polk®, and Boston Acoustics®. I explored their product lines, consumed their brochures and spent hours upon hours in stereo shops where I never spent any money cuz I didn't have any.

What inspired me was the manufacturer's pursuit of excellence. Like I said, I didn't really understand why it inspired me so much, I just knew it did. And yes, on one level it seemed kind of superficial to relentlessly pursue the ever-elusive "ultimate listening experience" with speakers and stereo equipment when the world had so many burgeoning problems. It's just another kind of Rolex watch. Shouldn't I be helping Mother Teresa instead?

But on the other hand, art is art. Beauty is beauty. You can only make the world a better place by creating more of it.

Is the world a better place when the English Concert playing the Four Seasons sounds like a real chamber quartet right in your living room?

Yessir. Sure does ease the stress of a long day, that's for sure. For me personally, it's the best kind of exploratory Renaissance time.

Maybe you should follow your heart, pursue that passion, and allow the answers to the Big Questions to unfold by themselves. And who knows, you might just find that in the process of selling truly excellent audio equipment to doctors and lawyers, you're also able to rub a few coins together and give them to Mother Teresa.

Maybe Melvin wearing a Rolex actually generates more wealth, through economic alchemy, for him to give to the poor than he would if he were not wearing one. (The world often does work that way. Wealth is not a zero-sum game.)

Maybe It's Not Either/Or

In the list of alternatives above, #7 was the option that really made sense to me. I said to myself: "Self, you've been given a certain amount of talent, a certain number of gifts, a certain amount of time, and a certain amount of freedom. Are you going to take the 'safe' path and do something predictable and restrictive? Or are you going to choose a path where you at least have a fighting chance at fulfilling your own personal vision in the world?"

I knew that I was either going to be working to fulfill my vision or somebody else's.

In Option #7, money serves *you*. Not the other way around. And *that* is the difference between loving money and using it. You shouldn't use people and love money. You should love people and use money.

Put the people first.

Some People Get Memos. That's Great. So What Do I Do Now?

I'M WRITING THIS AT THE VERY beginning of 2021, having just lived through a year rocked by a global pandemic in ways that most of us could have never imagined.

It was Friday, March 13, 2020. I was hosting a live workshop at my home office when my personal assistant, Lorena, informed me that a client urgently needed to use a "911 coupon" and speak with me immediately. I called him right away. He ran a tennis instruction facility and the state of Illinois had just shut down all such businesses due to COVID-19.

That was the moment I knew life on Earth was about to get really interesting.

I literally woke up the next day with thousands of clients whose businesses were going up in flames, and I also needed to extricate myself from my own financial tailspin. For example, I had already sold 100 tickets to a live event, which was scheduled to be held in just two months.

Suddenly, people were hanging on my every word. They needed answers because businesses they had spent years building were suddenly teetering on the edge of collapse.

And I did not have the answers. I had never lived through anything like this, either. Yet—I felt strangely equipped to deal with this bizarre situation and walk people through it anyway.

I started hosting webinars and Zoom calls. My clients and I began sifting through the gigantic mess and figuring out what might be done. It seemed like every situation was yet another great unknown. But I would always ask for wisdom, and somehow it always seemed like it was forthcoming.

I gave my listeners a "Pandemic Assignment." I said: "After you wake up every single day, start your Renaissance time by sitting down with your notebook and cup of coffee. Say to the Head Office:

> OK. You've got my attention now.
> What do you want me to know?

"Then listen. And write whatever comes. Do not edit. Do not think. Do not compose. Just capture what comes next.

"Then follow through with it—whatever it may be."

In that moment, I felt like all the folks on that Zoom meeting were saying, "OK, Perry, maybe I wouldn't have done that last week, but you're on. I'll do it."

A few months later I heard from one of my best students, Tim Berthold: ex-Navy, runs a nutrition company. Married just before the pandemic hit, with a baby on the way. His daughter was born during the pandemic, right after the family moved from the East Coast to the West Coast.

He said, "Perry, one of the best things I got this year was that question you gave us: 'OK, Head Office, you've got my attention now. What do you want me to know?'

"The memo that kept coming back was I have a gift for nurturing young protégé managers in my company, and I need to build into them."

This opened a brand-new conversation thread we'd never had before. It continued for several months. It opened vistas for scaling his company and adding new product lines. Tim is now capitalizing on an entire dimension of his personal skills that I don't believe he was recognizing before.

A great many entrepreneurs not only survived but thrived in the hideous year of 2020. And when I asked these people "What was the #1 factor in maintaining your sanity?" they gave me two consistent answers: Renaissance Time and memos from the Head Office. That extra push of confidence, the wind at your back, that reassurance in the face of uncertainty, often makes all the difference when the chaos is spinning hard.

As I write this on January 6, 2021, it is more than certain we are in for a turbulent decade. The pandemic will subside, but other challenges will follow.

The best times to plant a tree are 20 years ago and today.

Likewise, the best time to cultivate your listening ear is . . . today.

The online supplement includes a free "Spiritual Perception Profile" that helps you discern how you (already) most easily capture inspiration and hear the Head Office: www.perrymarshall.com/morememos.

You've reached the end of the book...
but this is not the end!

There's a good deal more to read, watch, listen to, and participate in. I put the remainder of the book online because the web is far more conducive to ongoing conversations, comments from readers, and explorations. You can access this at **www.perrymarshall.com/morememos**.

HERE'S AN APPETIZER:

Appendix 1 is "Warning About the Dark Side: From Driving to Flying." It chronicles my own journey, including a number of misadventures. I candidly share with you some of the things that can go wrong with memos and some tragic wipeouts I've witnessed along the way. You'll hear more of my own spiritual journey with several jumping-off points, including audio and video resources.

Appendix 1 is included in the book and provided online to facilitate questions, answers and discussion.

Appendix 2 through 4 are online only:

Appendix 2 is "For Christians Who Are a Little Freaked Out By This." Even though I'm a Christian, I sometimes get the most pushbacks from other Christians who have myriad objections, theological concerns, and in many cases their own negative experiences.

You'll discover several experiences I had that sharpened my discernment and clued me into the delicate nature of honing your listening ear.

Appendix 3 is called "Is It Ethical to Pay for Memos?" I pay the memos people on my team, and it's a wonderful thing that they are available in the exact same way that any other professional (doctor, pastor, counselor, graphic designer) is. I have a chaplain and intercessor on retainer in my own company. However, some people are extremely uncomfortable with this.

Here I show there is a long history behind this question, which most people have never heard, and offer you some new ways to think about the spiritual resources you avail yourself of.

Appendix 4, "About the Contributors," includes up-to-date information about the people featured in this book. As I said in the beginning, virtually no story in this book is anonymous, and this will enable you to find out more about who these interesting people are.

The online supplements for this book also include the Spiritual Perception Profile, plus links to many of the books and resources mentioned in this book, as well as additional YouTube channels and podcasts.

You'll also get access to live memo sessions on a donation basis so you can experience what so many other people in this book describe.

Access the online appendices, audios, and videos at www.perrymarshall.com/morememos.

Appendix 1

Warning about the Dark Side: From Driving to Flying

MY FRIEND JEFF TIDEMAN ONCE TOOK me for a ride in his Cessna 172 and allowed me to take over as pilot for most of the trip—except takeoff and landing. It was scary—and exhilarating!

When I first took the controls, the plane became wobbly and unstable. Every adjustment I made threw us off balance, pitching forward or back or rolling sideways. The experience was incredibly disorienting.

Taking control of the plane seemed like it should be similar to driving a car, but when you're driving, the horizon isn't bobbing up and down above and below your dashboard, tilting crazily to the right and left. Because when you drive, you can only do four things: Go faster or slower and turn left or right. You're moving on *one* axis of rotation.

But when you fly an airplane, you can do eight things: you can go faster or slower; you can yaw (turn left or right); you can pitch (tilt forward or backward); and you can roll (to the left or the right). *Three* axes of rotation.

Going from one axis of rotation to three is *exponentially* more complex!

Every move I made had the opposite effect of what I expected. So, I would pull some other lever—and make the problem WORSE. Of course, I knew that Jeff's little Cessna could become a burning pyre of twisted wreckage in literally 30 seconds if I lost control—which seemed *soooo* easy to do. The instantaneous instability made me feel very insecure.

The one thing that saved us was Jeff's steady hand. He knew exactly what he was doing and how much leeway to give me. (In fact, Jeff even *built* airplanes!)

Learning to look for memos from the Head Office will be a little like my disorienting Cessna flight. When you go from "I'm just going to live my life by sight and instruments" to asking the Head Office what to do about your bad employee or your sales problem or the fight you're having with your spouse, you introduce more dimensions to the equation.

It means there will be more ways to crash. More ways to get it wrong and faster.

But it's also the only way to fly.

Cars don't fly. If you want to fly, you need an airplane. So, if you want to *hear* from the Head Office, then commit yourself to hearing as keenly as possible. Because a person who hears wrong much of the time can be downright dangerous. Making a big decision based on a bad memo can have big consequences.

While I believe (and have *seen*) that anyone of any religious belief— or no religious belief at all—can GET helpful or even life-changing memos, I know from experience that there can also be a very real dark side to memos. And I feel it's my duty to warn you about that darkness.

In the late 1990s a men's movement called Promise Keepers gained a huge following. Bill McCartney, then the football coach at the University of Colorado, held some events and men started flocking to them. Pretty soon, the organization was filling stadiums. I went to several, and they were great.

In 1997, hundreds of thousands of men descended on Washington, DC, for a giant Promise Keeper's gathering on the Mall. I'll never forget how Bill got up on the last day of that meeting and announced, "God told me to make all Promise Keepers meetings free from now on, so that *everybody* can come!"

The crowd cheered!

But I distinctly remember thinking: *Bill, are you sure that was from God? People don't value what they don't pay for. Besides, most people can afford to come to these things anyway.*

At the time, the entrance fee to a Promise Keepers event was about $70, and that included bottled water and a sack lunch. This seemed a perfectly reasonable fee for food and an entire day of activity, and it allowed the organization to pay for the stadium, speakers, musicians and administration. Promise Keepers could have easily publicized the availability of scholarships for guys who couldn't afford the entrance fee. Most men could surely ask a friend to help if they really wanted to go but couldn't afford that fee.

When Promise Keepers made their events free, the entire organization *immediately* collapsed into a financial tailspin. It was suddenly dependent on a few major donors (hundreds of thousands of people times $70 is a lot of dinero!) and paltry margins of selling books and music. Within months, one of the biggest men's movements of the decade was *over*. Promise Keepers largely vanished, although the organization has made attempts to regroup in recent years.

I don't know whether Bill's memo was a malevolent voice or a bad burrito. I don't know if Bill acted on a sudden impulse or deliberated over it for months. But there's nothing you could say to convince me it was the actual Head Office who told him to stop charging entrance fees for events. It was one of the most tragic leadership decisions I've ever seen. I don't know any of the people involved in that move, but my guess is it was a hasty decision that was not properly vetted.

AVOIDING MEMO MISCOMMUNICATION

In my own life, I try to carefully consider any memos that would lead to major changes and seek affirmation from more than one source. This past summer, Vivian Hearn, the woman who told me I was working on a math problem in 2003—the one that became the 80/20 curve—suddenly started telling me, "Perry you need to re-examine your org chart." She was talking about my company, but she was also talking about the positioning of numerous other people in my life. She insisted, "You're going to be making some major changes very soon and you need to listen to the Head Office *very* carefully and examine every position."

About the same time, one or two other prophetic people independently started telling me the same thing. Not long after that, a couple of unusual problems popped up. So, I took a personal retreat for a weekend for the express purpose of rethinking how I wanted to run my team.

Four days later I got on the phone with a key staff member in my company. I asked him, "Are these recent issues just symptoms of the particular moment we're in, or is there a bigger problem here?"

He said, "It's a bigger problem. I no longer have the interest or inclination to do this job anymore. I want to start doing something else."

Because of the memos I had received, I had been thinking this person would need to be removed from the job, and I had been nervous that this would turn into a contentious conversation. So, I was elated when the two of us painlessly agreed, in the space of about two minutes, that it was time to start looking for his replacement. This man had been a fixture in the company, and I would have never given a moment's thought to actually replacing him if Vivian had not bent my ear about it.

Even so, I took the time to assess the situation and do my best to confirm the memo before acting on Vivian's suggestion. You need to know that things can go wrong with memos and take steps to head off potential problems.

Avoid pitfalls like these.

- **Rushed actions.** If you get a memo about making a major change, seek confirmation. Don't act rashly without a second or third confirmation from somewhere else.
- **Manipulators.** Some prophetic people may try to manipulate and control you because they hear well and you don't, so they think it's their job to tell you what to do. That is *never* a good sign. Some people put their words in God's mouth . . . instead of God's words in their mouth. (Think about that for a minute. That's a heavy bite to chew on.) When prophetic people are operating appropriately, they offer their words provisionally, with humility. They will almost always say something like, "You need to check this out with the Head Office and with other people" or "Hold this with an open hand." Be wary of people who do *not* convey this attitude and seem like they're trying to control you.
- **Inappropriate relationships.** A good memo can provoke a powerful sense of intimacy and safe vulnerability, providing space for less-than-appropriate relationships to form. Avoid prophetic people you sense have bad boundaries.
- **Needy prophets.** Disengage if you ever start to feel like a prophet needs you to feed their ego or appease their insecurities, or if they make you feel their words come with an "IOU" attached.
- **Too many prophets.** Prophetic words don't trump everything else. They do not substitute for good administrators or accountants or scientists or teachers. An organization with lots of prophets and no administrators is a tilt-a-whirl.
- **The dark side.** Memos can absolutely come from the dark side, and there is a dark side. Stay away from mediums, astrologers and fortune-tellers.

TRUTH AND LOVE

Ultimately, memos from the Head Office are about truth. And I don't believe that truth is a memo, or a creed, or even a religion. Truth is a person. That person is LOVE. My experience with that person is Jesus. I believe that the fullest human expression of love was Jesus, love incarnate.

And love is the highest truth.

You can argue that Jesus' followers have perverted his message of love for the last 20 centuries, and you will be right—but you can't deny that he *was* love. He loved so much he was willing to die to prove it. You simply can't dispute that. He WAS love.

And for those of us who follow him, he IS and always will be Love.

And I firmly believe *the further you stray from love, the further you stray from truth*. They are inseparable. And the world needs more of both now more than ever.

Don't worry, you don't have to label yourself a Christian to follow LOVE. You don't have to go to church to follow love. You don't have to recite a creed or perform a ritual to follow love.

You can start with this: "God is Love."

I have a client named Chris who might get a PTSD reaction if anyone tried to drag him into any religious belief system. Yet he will still assure you the best part of his day is when he walks his dog to a park bench by a pond and meditates on *Love* with a capital L.

I seek my memos from people who are disciples of Jesus. His favorite disciple said, "Every spirit which testifies that Jesus came to earth in the flesh and is the son of God, giving Him the credit, is of God."

Avoid mediums. Many are there to put themselves in the spotlight—not to bring honor to God. Shopping for psychics and fortune-tellers is like fishing in the open ocean from a canoe. A squall can come out of nowhere and wipe you out.

I Know What a Lot of Folks Are Thinking . . .

"Oh, great. I just read this inspiring book about tapping into divine inspiration and now Perry's giving me a pitch for Jesus. Ugh, I really should have seen this coming. Reminds me of my smug sanctimonious Bible-thumper brother-in-law. The one who cheated on my sister for six years. I could throw that bastard through a plate-glass window.

"Yeah . . . thanks. But no thanks."

Boy do I ever get that. My dad was a pastor at a large church, and both of my parents were humiliated in front of 2,000 people because my mom had bipolar disorder. Dad had taken my mom to a psychiatrist, and the psychiatrist prescribed medication, which worked. But the church leaders accused her of "rebellion" and "sin." Then they demoted my dad from his job because psychiatrists were off-limits.

It was our family's trip to hell and back. I will never forget what it was like to experience those dark days with all that was swirling around us. (You can hear the full story at https://youtu.be/WyCi4mehe2k or https://tinyurl.com/bipolarstory. This specific incident starts about 23:30 into the video.)

My coauthor of this book, John Fancher, says: "I personally think Christians should take a few hundred years off from *saying* 'Jesus' and just BE Jesus. And shut up about it. That's the Saint Francis in me."

George MacDonald, a famous Christian speaker and writer in the 19th century, said, "It's better to have not known about Him than to learn Him wrong."

I've taken multiple trips through the religious hypocrisy smorgasbord buffet and wolfed down second, third and fourth helpings, with dessert. I've seen the most nightmarish *and* the most sublime faces of faith communities. The same church people who confronted my dad took very good care of us when he was dying of cancer three years later.

So, if this section is making you queasy—if you've been on the receiving end of religious hypocrisy and control—I understand. I've had to sort out a *lot* of bitterness toward so-called religious people. If you've been hurt, I propose that you issue the following request to the Head Office.

Start by saying:

*I'm not interested in my **idea** of the Head Office; I'm asking to hear from the **actual** Head Office.*

Anyone at any stage of growth who belongs to *any* belief system—or none at all—can make that request.

Then ask:

Show me where and when people showed me a fake Jesus. And show me what the real Jesus looks like.

Start there. See where that request takes you.

This next step is *very* important. You need to forgive.

Remember all the stories in this book about forgiveness? Like Bonnie Kim screaming at God about her client while driving on the Los Angeles freeway? Or the guy who forgave the person at 9:20 a.m. and his lawsuit got settled at 9:24 a.m.? Everyone I've ever known who was abused by religion has needed to forgive. The story of my mom and dad and his pastor boss is a story of forgiveness.

CONSIDER THE SOURCE

It's a big world out there, and there is no lack of prophets of every maturity level—good, mediocre, bad. There are also plenty of psychics, mediums, oracles, seers, energy healers, etc. Trying to listen to all of them is like climbing into a Cessna 172, taking off and then twisting every lever you can think of. Please exercise great caution about the prophetic because careful curation is essential.

Soliciting memos is no different than sourcing any other kind of power or talent. The average employee, the average accountant, the average marketing manager, the average baseball coach is frankly not all that good. Lawyers have bar associations, doctors have medical boards, and plumbers and electricians need certifications. But there is no world standard for certifying prophetic people, so you must take great care.

If you receive a memo, *always ask:* "Is the memo really from the Head Office? Or is it coming from some other source?"

That is a very important question. Not trivial. Can't skip over this one.

I have one relative who suffered severe migraine headaches and was slammed with depression every time she made love to her husband. (In other words, one of the two was miserable all the time.) Those migraines suddenly and dramatically disappeared after a prayer counseling session revealed that her grandfather had committed himself to Masonry. After the power of Masonry was broken, she was set free from some terrible reactions and feelings. It was as if a portal to negativity in her life was shut tight.

I have another relative who was tormented for years with addictive behaviors, including cocaine addiction, and a string of toxic relationships, including a physically abusive husband. It all ended after a prayer session broke the power of Wicca. Several other family members had been deeply involved.

Some forces in the spiritual world are malevolent, so when I'm requesting memos, the way that I make sure I'm dealing with the Head Office is by going through Jesus—the man who split time in half, BC and AD.

Here's a story I tell in my "Seven Great Lies of Organized Religion" email series (available at www.coffeehousetheology.com).

A certain man threatened the Religious Gestapo, who in turn convinced the Roman government that He was a threat to them, too.

His followers were disappointed that He didn't overthrow the Romans and declare himself King, like the Messiah was supposed to do. So, they abandoned Him.

The ancient Romans perfected what was possibly the cruellest form of torture ever devised by man: crucifixion. They would drive spikes into their victim's ankles and wrists, smashing his nerves. He would hang there in blinding sheets of pain, slowly suffocating and dehydrating for days, until he finally expired.

Not only that, but vultures would also come and start taking chunks of flesh before the victim was even dead. If any of us ever witnessed a crucifixion, we'd be seeing a psychiatrist for months just to deal with our own trauma.

All this was highly calculated. Crucifixion meant: *Rome is 100% in charge, ladies and gentlemen. And if any of you EVER forget this one fact, this is what will happen to you.*

Jesus was whipped and beaten, literally beyond recognition, then nailed to a cross between two common criminals.

One of these criminals was cursing and shouting at Him in a fit of rage: "HEY! If you're the KING, why don't you get yourself down from there! And US, TOO!!!"

The other guy went along with this . . . for a little while.

But he saw that Jesus wasn't hurling insults at his torturers. Instead, He was asking God to forgive them (?!).

He sobered up. He said to the other criminal, "Hey dude, you and I are here because we deserve it. But this man Jesus has done nothing wrong."

Then he said to Jesus, "Remember me when you take charge of your Kingdom."

Jesus simply replied, "Today you'll be with me in Paradise."

Stop the camera.

What you have here, in this brief conversation, is a snapshot of the entire world.

You have two criminals who have gotten themselves into a horrendous, awful mess. And you have the Son of God, who has not only chosen to live with us in our world of pain and suffering but has personally taken all of it upon his own shoulders.

Even though he is completely innocent.

One thief refuses to accept any responsibility for his actions.

He's unwilling to admit that he created the very mess that he's in.

He lives in denial until the bitter end. He grits his teeth and dies in his sin.

The other thief comes clean. He recognizes that Jesus possesses divine authority. He admits his guilt. He is required to do nothing, other than to let go of his pride.

He asks for forgiveness.

Forgiveness granted.

Jesus' pardon doesn't make the cross or the agony go away. But finally, the struggle ceases and this man crosses the Great Divide. The intense pain dissolves and he steps into a New World, architected by God Himself—with renewed body and soul.

That's a picture of the entire world, right there.

You and I are in this mess together, and we've all contributed to it.

We've all rejected God in some way or another, we've all committed some kind of crime, and we all experience suffering.

The situation is what it is.

So, we have a simple choice: Accept the fact that God has suffered with us—or mock him and be furious because the suffering exists in the first place.

Which way do you want it?

Readers of this book are most likely all over the place as far as religious faith goes. You may have reservations about Jesus, and that's OK. If you'd like to explore this much more deeply, go to www.perrymarshall.com/spirituality and register for the email series. See how deep the rabbit hole goes.

But as I close this book, I would like to focus on one of the Bible's most beautiful passages. It's from the book of John, chapter 1:

> In the beginning was the Word, and the Word was with God, and the Word was God. He was with God in the beginning. Through him all things were made; without him nothing was made that has been made. In him was life, and that life was the

light of all mankind. **The light shines in the darkness, and the darkness has not overcome it.**

The Word became flesh and lived among us. We have seen his glory, the glory of the one and only Son, who came from the Father, full of grace and truth.

Every bit of this is beautiful. In fact, it's sublime poetry. But I want to focus on the sentence in bold: **The light shines in the darkness, and the darkness has not overcome it.**

No darkness is more powerful than Christ. If you are a follower of Christ, you have the keys to the kingdom. All you have to do is say, "God, I want to be a Christ follower." And then start reading the book of John.

If you're not sure about Christ, then do this: Just say, "God, whoever you are, I don't want my *idea* of God, I want the real, ultimate, most powerful God, the way God IS. Even if the way God is seems strange to me. God, if you're real, show me."

Read the book of John and listen to how it speaks to you—especially to your intuitive, creative side.

In this book I am imparting to you—and inviting you into—my connection with the Head Office. Because I want you to have that, too. I want everyone to have it.

Index

About the Cover

EIGHT YEARS AGO, CO-AUTHOR JOHN FANCHER and I visited what our friends described as "the thin places of Ireland"—areas where the veil between heaven and Earth is thinner. Both of us were profoundly transformed by that trip. Each time we return, the magic begins again.

In December 2020, just ahead of the new year, Ireland relaxed their travel restrictions for a time. My 16-year-old son Zander and I escaped COVID lockdown in Chicago to Ireland's west coast. We took these photographs there.

The front cover shows the lone window of the Gallarus Oratory near Ballyferriter Village on the Dingle Peninsula. The Oratory is a tiny stone church built 1,200 years ago using only stones, no mortar. It stands intact today and has given both physical and spiritual shelter to innumerable pilgrims across the centuries.

The back-cover photograph was taken just north of Clogher Beach near Dún Chaoin, the westernmost town in Europe. Zander is seen walking toward the spray as it rises with Clogher Head in the distance.

About the Authors

Perry Marshall is one of the most expensive business strategists in the world. He is endorsed in *Forbes* and *Inc.* magazines and has written eight books. At London's Royal Society, he announced the world's largest science research challenge, the $10 million Evolution 2.0 Prize. His reinvention of the Pareto Principle is published in *Harvard Business Review*, and his Google book laid the foundations for the $100 billion pay-per-click industry. He has a degree in electrical engineering and lives with his family in Chicago.

John Fancher is a business consultant, musician, and part-time pastor. John has written for Infusionsoft, Richard Koch, Magnetic Marketing, and over 100 other clients. He lives in Chicago with his wife of over 25 years, Jay. They have three children, Dylan, Symphony, and Reed.

Made in the USA
Middletown, DE
08 April 2023